The
Commandments
of Christ

The Commandments of Christ

A Topical Study
of Christian Discipleship

Robert C. Beasley

P&R
P U B L I S H I N G
P.O. BOX 817 • PHILLIPSBURG • NEW JERSEY 08865-0817

Page design by Tobias Design
Typesetting by Michelle Feaster

Printed in the United States of America

Library of Congress Cataloging-in-Publication Data
Beasley, Robert C., 1938–
    The commandments of Christ : a topical study of Christian
discipleship / Robert C. Beasley.
        p.   cm.
    Includes bibliographical references.
    ISBN 0-87552-171-1
    1. Christian life—Biblical teaching—Study and teaching.
2. Bible. N.T.—Study and teaching. I. Title.
BS2545.C48B43 1999
241.5—dc21   98-50068

To

George and Londa Miladin

with special thanks to
John Frame

Contents

Preface

Jesus says in John 14:15, "If you love me, you will obey what I command." For the loyal follower of Christ, obedience to the Lord is axiomatic. If someone has no desire to obey the One he claims is his Lord, he has no Lord. But the person who is overwhelmed by the grace of his Savior will long to obey Christ out of heartfelt gratitude. And that means following the commands of Christ.

Jesus compared His commandments to a yoke. But this yoke does more than put people to work or keep their nose to the grindstone. Christ's yoke brings joy to the redeemed soul. He says in Matthew 11:28–30, "Come to me, all you who are weary and burdened, and I will give you rest. Take my yoke upon you and learn from me, for I am gentle and humble in heart, and you will find rest for your souls. For my yoke is easy and my burden is light."

The Lord's commandments should not be viewed as drudgery or approached in fear. Amazingly, the child of God finds them to be a source of utter joy and rest. As the Spirit of Christ graciously strengthens and encourages us in our weaknesses, we receive power to keep His commands.

This work of the Spirit does not relieve us of accountability, to be sure, for we must all stand before Christ's judgment seat (2 Cor. 5:10). But it will be a judgment yielding His gracious rewards, not condemnation.

But what does Christ command us to do? If we don't know that, we cannot very well honor Him with our lives. Happily, we are not left to guess at what pleases Christ. His commands and those of His immediate ambassadors—the apostles—are laid out for us in the entire New Testament. Indeed, all of the commandments of the Old and New Testaments are the commandments of Christ, for all of the Bible is His Word and testifies to His lordship.

A few years ago, I taught two separate classes on this subject. I gathered up all of the direct commandments I could find from the mouth of our Lord in the Gospels and in Acts, and from the pens of His apostles. (By the way, the weight of the commands from each of those sources is the same. No less importance should be given to apostles' words. Their commands are of God just as surely as are Christ's.)

Next, I organized the direct commandments I found into separate topics, and listed the commands within those topics as they appear in the Bible, book by book. The positive feedback I received from those studies prompted me to put the study into book form to help individuals and groups read, meditate on, pray through, discuss, and grow in obedience to the commandments of Christ.

It would be a mistake to think that we receive moral guidance from the direct commands alone. This book does not replace the whole of Scripture, which points to the One we serve and wish to emulate in all righteousness and holiness. But the topical format found here can help us to focus on specific areas of Christian morality in a profound way.

I have added the Ten Commandments to this New Testament study in order to show how the New Testament commands fit under the Decalogue's summary of the law given to the Hebrews. The whole Bible is one unit. We understand the Old Testament by the New, and the New by the Old.

I have also added a chapter entitled "The Law and the Gospel" to the original study. There is much confusion between these two components of God's revelation to us, and we need to have each clearly defined in our thinking. Please study that section carefully. After all, this book on the law of Christ would be pointless if it were not for the gospel of Christ. Only as our eyes are fixed on the Author and Perfecter of our faith will we have the motivation, courage, and strength to live in obedience to the commandments of Christ.

Tips for Individual Study

A key element to any study of God's Word is meditation. When we chew upon the Word of God, rather than just reading it in a cursory fashion, we invite the Holy Spirit to apply God's Word to our hearts and lives. This is particularly important when we want Him to change our attitudes and actions, which we need always. So study each verse prayerfully and carefully.

I have added to each topic "Study Questions and Exercises," more verses to ponder, a memorization verse, and space for a personal action plan. Making use of those elements will contribute greatly to the success of your study. If you are studying with a group, doing these exercises in advance will help the group save time for discussion. You may want to enter your answers in a separate notebook.

As you study and meditate on each verse, hold it up against your own life and experience. Ask yourself what consequences have resulted from disobeying the verse's teaching, either in your own life or in the lives of others you know. Conversely, what have been the rewards of obedience? As you proceed, you should begin to see a pattern emerge. Disobedience ultimately results in pain, regret, and hardship, while obedience leads ultimately to joy, peace, and rest. This is because all sin—lack of conformity to God's law—turns out to be a trap the sinner sets for himself. As Proverbs 5:22 says, "The evil deeds of a wicked man ensnare him; the cords of his sin hold him fast." Far from being restrictive, the joyful reception and Spirit-empowered keeping of God's law actually frees us from this bondage of sin to be the people God wants us to be.

Finally, and of supreme importance, we need to put Christ's commandments into practice in our daily lives. The writer to the Hebrews says in 5:14, "Solid food is for the mature, who by constant use have trained themselves to distinguish good from evil." The mature Christian not only knows the Word of God but also learns to put it into practice. In this way he proves the Word of God to be true. Jesus said in Luke 7:35, "Wisdom is proved right by all her children." In other words, God's wisdom—His way of right living—is proved true by its results. The proof is in the pudding.

The Westminster Shorter Catechism Question 1 asks, "What is the chief end of man?" The answer: "Man's chief end is to glorify God and to enjoy him forever." I believe that God's glory and our joy are two sides to the same coin. We glorify God by enjoying Him, and He is glorified in our joy. How do we enjoy God and thereby glorify Him? By keeping His commandments and by allowing our faith—expressed in obedience—to overflow into thanksgiving for what He has done.

Tips for Group Leaders

Christ's commandments in a topical format offer a wonderful medium for group dynamics and discussion. Since none of us has kept His precepts perfectly, all of us can think of our own imperfections and the results of our disobedience or obedience.

If you are leading a group, you might want to use a topical Bible to bring in additional background verses throughout Scripture that help highlight the topic. Examples from Scripture and from your own life are very useful in getting the conversation flowing. Of course, much will depend on the size of your group and the amount of time you have to discuss each topic.

It is extremely important to encourage the members of your group to read each chapter in advance, meditate on the verses, and complete the exercise portions of each study before coming to class. Such preparation will enable them to develop their own insights and to share them more readily with others, facilitating discussion. You may also want to encourage group members to record their answers to the Study Questions and Exercises in a separate notebook.

I have arranged this volume into 13 individual study sessions that fit into a 13-week Sunday school quarter. The chapters listing New Testament commands contain two topical segments. In such a format, and when only one hour or less is available for class discussion, I would recommend that leaders select one or two verses from each topic before class that are most representative of the others, and that discussion surround those selected verses. Discussion might also center on one or more of the Study Questions and Exercises at the end of each chapter or segment.

As mentioned above, we sinners become aware of our own weaknesses as the Word of God shines the light of truth upon them. Group members should be urged to share their difficulties and struggles and perhaps how the Holy Spirit and Scripture have helped them turn defeat into victory. Where group members have not found victory over some sin, discussion can often evoke confession and a request for prayer and help.

Each moment of our lives we find ourselves in situations where God's law needs to be applied—at home, at work, in the grocery store, at school, and on the freeway. How has the application of God's law made a difference in the lives of your group members? What have been the results of obedience and disobedience? How has your response to God's law affected interpersonal relationships, or the attitudes of your heart?

All of the chapters of this volume share a link to God's law. Therefore, I have listed below some questions that apply to each discussion, regardless of the topic:

1. In what ways could disobedience to this command result in a trap you set for yourself? (See Prov. 1:17–19; 5:21–23; 6:9–11; 7:21–23; and 20:17 for examples of self-entrapment.)

2. What pressures in our society might tempt us to disobey this command?

3. How is a person's joy heightened and made firm by keeping this commandment?

4. Could violating this command become a habit? If so, how can we break the patterns of habitual sin in our lives?

5. In what ways will obedience to this command set you free? In other words, how is Paul's statement in Romans 8:1–6 re-

alized in your daily life? (That's where he says that "the law of the Spirit of life has set me free from the law of sin and death.")

6. Each chapter's list of verses contains numerous opportunities for questions. Before class, review the Bible quotations and ask yourself some questions:

   a. Who in Scripture reflects the positive or negative aspect of this specific command?

   b. Why do you suppose God commands us to do this?

   c. How can we best exemplify obedience to this command in our daily lives?

   d. What can I do to obey Christ more completely in regard to this command?

For those who are willing to commit to a longer time frame for study, such as a full year or three quarters in a home fellowship or small group, the time for group discussion can be greatly expanded, and the benefits magnified. In the studies I have led on these topics, the problem has not been getting people to open up. In fact it has been just the opposite. Keep the conversation on course. Focus on the results of wisdom living—right living by the grace of God. This will assure that those younger in the faith will be led from self-dependence to God-dependence, from living by sight to living by faith. It is my prayer that class members will be encouraged to begin their

own study of God's law in their families, teaching their young-
sters the joy of obedience.

The impact of a topical study of any kind can be dramatic.
But to study Christ's commands in a topical format is extremely powerful. I pray that as you study, meditate, and practice the commands of Christ, God will mold and shape you and
your group into the persons He wants you to be, and bring you
the joy, peace, and rest that is known only by children of God
who delight in their heavenly Father.

Chapter *1*

The Law and the Gospel

THE LAW

Paul states in Romans 6:14 that we "are not under law, but under grace." Does he mean that the Old Testament moral law based on the Ten Commandments is no longer in effect now that Christ has come? Can we Christians disregard God's law and live any way we please, as some think today, because we are "under grace"? Paul answers in verse 15, "God forbid!" (KJV). His emphasis in Romans 6 is not on doing away with the law but on the grace of God that empowers us to keep the law. While the ceremonial law of the Old Testament—such as the slaughter of bulls and goats—was abolished by Christ's ultimate sacrifice, which those sacrifices foreshadowed, the moral law of God will not be abrogated, "until heaven and earth pass away" (Matt. 5:18 NASB).

God gave His people the law for three basic reasons. First, *He wanted to show them who He was,* what their Creator was like. He wanted them to know the absolute holiness of their God. In this way God's law was to restrain sin in society by providing a ground for all moral laws and ethical decisions.

Second, *He wanted to show the Israelites who they were*—sinners who could not keep His law and so were doomed to destruction unless they cried out for His mercy. In other words, the law was to drive them to despair and to the need to beg for God's free salvation, which is by grace alone. The law, in all its

1

manifestations—moral, ceremonial, and civil—pointed to Christ in His three offices as Prophet, Priest, and King.

Third, the Old Testament law was given *to call out of the world a holy people.* God said in Leviticus 11:44, "Be holy, because I am holy." God wants His people—whether known as "Israelites" or "the church"—to reflect His glory and thereby glorify their Creator. In that way, the creature's happiness and enjoyment of life will be maximized. Conversely, to oppose God's law is to set a trap for oneself and to bring on ultimate disaster. But those who "listen to [wisdom] will live in safety and be at ease, without fear of harm" (Prov. 1:33).

This third and last use of the law is most important to us as God's children. One of my favorite verses of Scripture is Romans 8:28: "And we know that in all things God works for the good of those who love him, who have been called according to his purpose." The "all things" includes God's law. The goodness of God's law is expressed in at least four ways in Scripture.

(1) *The law is intended to be our delight as His children.* The psalmist said in Psalm 119:97, "Oh, how I love your law! I meditate on it all day long." Paul said in Romans 7:22, "For in my inner being I delight in God's law." (2) *The law of God is a gift of His grace.* Psalm 119:29 says, "Keep me from deceitful ways; be gracious to me through your law." (3) *God's law provides a way of life for the believer.* In Leviticus 18:5 God says, "Keep my decrees and laws, for the man who obeys them will live by them. I am the LORD." And again in Deuteronomy 8:3, "Man does not live on bread alone but on every word that comes from the mouth of the LORD." (4) *The law has been given for our benefit.* In Deuteronomy 10:12–13, Moses asks the rhetorical question, "And now, O Israel, what does the LORD your God ask of you but to fear the LORD your God, to walk in all his ways, to love him, to serve the LORD your God with all your heart and with all your soul, and to observe the LORD's commands and decrees that I am giving you today for your own good?"

But the law without grace is weak because of our sinful nature (Rom. 8:3). It can only command and demand, pronounce judgment or approval, expose our sin, and even incite us to more serious transgression. But it cannot justify us—make us right with God. The law cannot do anything to relieve our bondage to sin. What Paul meant by our being "under law" was first that we were really under the dominion of sin (Rom. 6:14); and second, being under the dictates of the ritual, ceremonial law of the Mosaic economy. The Christian is not "under law" in that sense. But we are "under law" in the sense that God's moral law will never pass away (Matt. 5:18). Now there is power available to us, however, a power to obey and a power that covers the penalty we deserve even when we do our best. It is the gospel of Jesus Christ.

THE GOSPEL

The scribes and Pharisees of Jesus' day were specialists in the law. But they didn't get the point! They thought that by closely adhering to the outward requirements of the law, they would endear themselves to God. He never intended that anyone could be saved by keeping the law (Rom. 3:20; Gal. 2:16). God knew that sinful men couldn't even come close.

The error of the scribes and Pharisees shouldn't surprise us. After all, every religion in the world—except one—insists that people can get right with God by their obedience to a set of standards. In other words, every other religion teaches salvation by one's own works. That's right, every one but one. The exception is biblical Christianity. But let's start at the beginning.

When God put Adam into the Garden of Eden, He gave the first man one commandment: "You must not eat from the tree of the knowledge of good and evil . . ." (Gen. 2:17). If Adam had complied, he and all those after him would have been blessed by his good work. But, as you know, he failed, and the entire human race was plunged into sin and ultimate destruction, into war with the Creator. Since Adam, "All [of us] have sinned and fall short of the glory of God" (Rom. 3:23). "There is no one righteous, not even one" (Rom. 3:11).

The human race has a real problem. But God, who is rich in mercy, sent His only Son—Jesus Christ—to live a perfectly righteous and sinless life, and then to suffer and die on a Roman cross to pay the penalty for the sins of His people. John 3:16 says that "God so loved the world that he gave his one and only Son, that whoever believes in him shall not perish but have eternal life." The apostle Paul adds, "For it is by grace [people like you and me] have been saved, through faith . . . it is the gift of God—not by works, so that no one can boast" (Eph. 2:8–9). Salvation is by faith alone in Christ, and not by works of the law.

There *is* one important sense in which we are saved by works, but those works are *not our works*. They are the works of our Savior, the God-man Jesus. We appropriate His righteousness by faith and His imputed righteousness is sufficient to cover all our sins and to cleanse us so that we are able to stand before a holy God. Just as His righteousness is imputed to us, our sins are imputed to Him. He bore them on the cross.

What about you? What or who are you trusting for salvation? If you are trusting in church membership, or in your own good works, or in anything other than the Lord Jesus, you are in deep trouble. The Bible says that the wrath of God abides on you (Rom. 1:18–23). There is only one way—one solution. "Believe in the Lord Jesus, and you will be saved" (Acts 16:31).

THE LAW AND THE CHRISTIAN

What then is the purpose of the law for the Christian, for those who have been saved by grace through faith alone in the Lord Jesus Christ? When a person repents of his sin and turns to Christ, he is given the gift of the Holy Spirit. The Spirit of

God comes to dwell within him, and that person is given a love for and a desire to please his Creator. The law then becomes a guide for holy and happy living. It is no longer perceived as our enemy, as something that must be kept perfectly to please God. The law becomes our guide and our friend.

We are saved by grace alone through faith alone in Christ alone, as the Reformers of the sixteenth century insisted. But ours is not a faith that stands alone. True saving faith is always followed by good works. James makes this clear in his epistle where he, in effect, defines saving faith:

> What good is it, my brothers, if a man claims to have faith but has no deeds? Can such faith [i.e., mere assent to a set of facts] save him? Suppose a brother or sister is without clothes and daily food. If one of you says to him, "Go, I wish you well; keep warm and well fed," but does nothing about his physical needs, what good is it? In the same way, faith by itself, if it is not accompanied by action, is dead. (James 2:14–17)

When saved, we are given a natural bent to want to please God, whereas before, our natural inclination was to displease God and to please our sinful selves. Do we always please and obey God perfectly? No; because we still struggle against sin, our obedience is far from what it should be. But because God has given us a new heart that is sensitive to His law, we can learn more and more to put to death our old sinful ways.

Many of our neighbors and acquaintances are still under the burden of the law. They still believe that they must produce their own merit—good works—in order to be saved. How we as Christians need to make known the gospel of Jesus Christ to them, that they too might view the law in a new light—as a friend and companion, and not as their enemy and slavemaster!

The law of the Ten Commandments and the larger Old Testament moral code, and of Christ and His apostles, is our guide to a joyful, fulfilling life on this earth, as well as rewards in heaven beyond what we can imagine. May God bless you as you grow in the knowledge and admonition of Him who has called you by His grace.

STUDY QUESTIONS AND EXERCISES

1. Read Genesis 15. Focusing on verse 6, what are we told is the basis for Abram's justification, the crediting or reckoning of righteousness to him? What did Abram believe? Does this mean that Abram was saved?

    a. Read Genesis 17. What does God now promise to Abram in verses 3–8? What does He give Abram immediately? What does God command Abraham to do in verse 10? Was this command before or after Abraham was saved?

    b. Read Genesis 22. Has God fulfilled His promise to Abraham? What does He command Abraham to do now? Does Abraham obey God?

    c. Read Romans 3:19–4:25. What light do these verses shed on the Genesis chapters?

    d. Read James 2:14–26. Are James' words in conflict with those of Paul in Romans? How is a person "justified by what he does and not by faith alone"?

2. Read Romans 8:1–17.

a. Why is there now no condemnation for some? (vv. 1–3)

b. What do you think is "the law of the Spirit of life" Paul is talking about in verse 2? How is it different from "the law of sin and death"?

c. Why can't a person be saved by keeping the law? (v. 3)

d. What has God done about this problem? (v. 3)

e. Are the law's requirements fully met in some people? Who? (v. 4)

f. What is one way we can know whether or not this is true of ourselves? (v. 4)

g. What relationship does the "sinful mind" have with God? (v. 7)

h. Who are the true "sons [children] of God"? (v. 14)

i. What other test of sonship is given in verse 16?

j. What benefits of sonship are listed in

(1) verse 6? _____ and _____.

(2) verse 11? _____.

(3) verse 17? _____.

3. Read Matthew 28:19–20. What command does Christ give there? To whom does it apply? Express the gospel in your own words.

More Verses to Ponder
Habakkuk 2:4; Acts 15:7–9; Ephesians 2:8–9; Hebrews 11:8–12

A Verse to Memorize
"But now a righteousness from God, apart from law, has been made known, to which the Law and the Prophets testify." (Rom. 3:21)

My Personal Action Plan to Be Able to Explain to Unbelievers the Gospel of Jesus Christ

1.

2.

3.

4.

Chapter 2

The Ten Commandments (1): Commandments 1-4

A SUMMARY OF THE WHOLE LAW

In Deuteronomy 6:4–5, following a restatement of the Ten Commandments in the preceding chapter, Moses summarized the entire moral law of God as he said to the people, "Hear, O Israel: The LORD our God, the LORD is one! Love the LORD your God with all your heart and with all your soul and with all your strength."

Jesus echoed Moses' summary in Mark 12:30 and then in verse 31 added, "The second [great commandment] is this, 'Love your neighbor as yourself.' There is no commandment greater than these."

In other words, all ten of the commandments God gave Moses at Mount Sinai are summarized in those two commandments. In the same way, the Ten Commandments (or "Decalogue," literally "ten words") summarize every other commandment of God in the Bible. They are the commandments of Christ just as surely as any command that came from Jesus' lips during His earthly ministry.

PERSPECTIVES ON THE WHOLE LAW

Another way to look at the Ten Commandments is as perspectives, principles, or different points of view on the whole of God's law. It's as if you were looking at your house from ten different angles: from the front yard, the driveway, the backyard, etc. The house is one object, but as you move around it, it takes on different shapes and you are better able to understand it by viewing it from different vantage points. Each commandment implies all of the others, but each has its separate role to play in viewing our obligation to love God.

James 2:10 says, "Whoever keeps the whole law and yet stumbles at just one point is guilty of breaking all of it." That's because the law is about one thing—loving the Lord your God with all of your heart, soul, and strength.

For example, suppose a man who claims to be a Christian commits adultery with another man's wife. He broke the tenth commandment by desiring or coveting her. He broke the ninth by seducing her with lies. He broke the eighth by stealing the woman from her rightful husband. He broke the seventh by disregarding the sanctity of sex and marriage. He broke the sixth commandment by despising the image of God in himself and others. He broke the fifth by disregarding the authoritative teaching of his church. He broke the fourth by denying the sovereignty of God over his life, particularly over his time. He broke the third as he claimed to love God and yet paid lip service to His law. He broke the second because he sought in a sinful act the pleasure that should only be sought in obedience to God's Word. Finally, the man broke the first commandment because he robbed His Creator of the honor and proper worship due Him.

So you see how every sin ultimately breaks all the commandments. They are interrelated, like a series of dominoes set on edge. Knock one down, and the rest follow in sequence. Any sin is ultimately cosmic rebellion against the Creator. Every sin is also an infinite sin because God, who is the violated party, is the infinite God. As you study the New Testament verses in this book, ask yourself at each verse, "How does this commandment relate to the Ten Commandments?" Or,

"Which of the Ten Commandments would be most grossly violated, or violated first, if I were to disobey this New Testament command?"

THE BREADTH OF THE DECALOGUE

It may have surprised you to read that the adulterous man above broke the fifth commandment by disregarding the authoritative teaching of his church. Doesn't the commandment simply say, "Honor your father and your mother"? Yes, and it is aimed directly at young people's obedience to their parents. But in a wider sense, the command applies to all earthly authority, whether in the home, the school, the church, or the government. These are authority structures God has placed on this earth as His representatives. We are to obey them if we fall under their jurisdiction.

An example of the breadth of the Ten Commandments is found in Matthew 5:21–30. There, Jesus tells us that the commandment against murder can be broken merely by being angry with someone. Likewise, the command against adultery is violated by lusting after another person in one's mind (Matt. 5:27–28). The act of murder or adultery is certainly worse than the thought, but sin is present nonetheless. As we have seen, the Ten Commandments are but summaries of the wider moral law God gives us throughout Scripture.

Interestingly, you may also notice that the fifth commandment is also the only one of the ten stated positively. (The fourth begins on a positive note, but its requirements are stated in negative terms.) But as the fifth might be stated negatively—"Do not disobey earthly authorities"—all the rest may be stated positively. For example, the tenth commandment, "You shall not covet" could be stated, "You shall be content with what is rightfully yours." In fact, it is stated much that way in Hebrews 13:5: "Keep your lives free from the love of money and be content with what you have."

SUMMARY OF THE TEN COMMANDMENTS

With these things in mind, let's look at each of the Ten Commandments in turn. Our very brief study of each will have three focal points: (1) The perspective through which the command leads us to see the whole law; (2) some of the thoughts and actions that the command prohibits; and (3) a synopsis of the behavior that the commandment requires.

As you study, either personally or with a group, try to think of some verses in the New Testament that may fall under each commandment. Please remember that my summaries are extremely brief. Many more prohibitions and requirements could be given for each.

For those wishing to study the Decalogue further, I have included a brief bibliography in the back of this book. I'm sure your pastor or group leader will also have some good suggestions for your continued reading.

This first of two chapters on the Decalogue will deal with the first four commandments. These are often seen as involving our relationship to God, while the final six are thought to deal with our relationship to other people. While this division offers some benefit, we should remember that all ten commandments are one cohesive unit summarizing the whole law.

The First Commandment

And God spoke all these words:

"I am the LORD your God, who brought you out of Egypt, out of the land of slavery. You shall have no other gods before me." (Ex. 20:1–3)

Perspective—Our Loyalty to God. Every person on earth owes loyalty to his or her Creator, and so all sin is ultimately disloyalty to God. As Christians, we must be particularly careful to give absolute priority to Him because, to paraphrase verse 2;

"He is the LORD our God, who brought us out of Satan's trap, out of slavery to sin and death" (see Rom. 8:2). We owe Christ our absolute loyalty, our unfailing love. That love for God, which He has shed abroad in our hearts by His Holy Spirit (Rom. 5:5), is our motivation for obedience to all His commands.

Prohibitions. We must not allow anything to divide our exclusive loyalty to God. Rival loyalties might include ethical rules beyond those of Scripture, occult practices such as astrology and witchcraft, secret societies that require unbiblical oaths of members, membership in apostate churches, or secular organizations that require behavior that opposes God's law. We must not give anyone or anything the worship and glory that is due only to the true God.

Requirements. First, we must turn away from sin to serve God according to His commandments. Next, we must deny ourselves and take up our cross daily and follow Christ (Luke 9:23). Third, we must separate ourselves from all associations, relationships, behaviors, and pastimes that divide our loyalty to the true and living God. Finally, "whether [we] eat or drink or whatever [we] do, [we should] do it all for the glory of God" (1 Cor. 10:31). We are to find our satisfaction and joy in the one true God, and not in any substitute.

The Second Commandment

> You shall not make for yourself an idol in the form of anything in heaven above or on the earth beneath or in the waters below. You shall not bow down to them or worship them; for I, the LORD your God, am a jealous God, punishing the children for the sin of the fathers to the third and fourth generation of those who hate me, but showing love to a thousand generations of those who love me and keep my commandments. (Ex. 20:4–6)

Perspective—Our Worship of God. Jesus told the woman at the well that "true worshippers will worship the Father in spirit and in truth" (John 4:23). This second commandment deals with the way in which we worship God. How do we know what pleases God in our worship and what does not? The principle that should regulate our corporate worship is to allow only what God has prescribed in His Word.

Prohibitions. The specific focus of the command prohibits idolatry in any form; that is, representing God by anything physical. God is spirit, mediated to us only by Christ. Any statue or icon that takes Christ's place is an insult to Him, and to we who are made in God's image. We must not attribute magical power to crucifixes or to sacraments or permit any program of worship invented by men. Nor must we attribute autonomous power to angels, to our own works, to money, or to any creature or invention of man. God alone has all the power, distributing it as He will.

Requirements. We are to worship God through our only Mediator, Jesus Christ, praying in His name with thanksgiving (Phil. 4:6). We are to read, hear, and put into practice the Word of God, so that we may not be guilty of false or superficial worship, which we are to detest. We are to attribute all power to God, and trust only in His providence to meet all of our needs.

The Third Commandment

> You shall not misuse the name of the Lord your God, for the Lord will not hold anyone guiltless who misuses his name. (Ex. 20:7)

Perspective—Our Integrity Before God. Many see this command as merely prohibiting the use of God's name as a swear word. But seen in a wider context, it condemns hypocrisy in any form. God's "name" is not merely a word. It is symbolic and revelatory of His whole being, His holy character and divine attributes. To take the name "Christian," and then to defile that name by professing to know Him when we do not, or to show disrespect in any way to our Creator, is to violate His name and to stand guilty before Him.

Prohibitions. We are not to take God's name upon ourselves—that is, to be known by His name—if we are not truly His. John says, "The man who says, 'I know [Christ],' but does not do what he commands is a liar, and the truth is not in him" (1 John 2:4). In essence, such a taking of Christ's name in vanity and hypocrisy is utter blasphemy, "for there is no other name under heaven given to men by which we must be saved" (Acts 4:12).

Requirements. "Whoever claims to live in [Christ] must walk as Jesus did" (1 John 2:6). We must walk circumspectly, hiding God's Word in our hearts that we do not take His name in vain and sin against Him (Ps. 119.11). We are to treat His name in reverential awe, and give it the honor it deserves—never trivializing it—as His ambassadors in this lost world. And we are to keep—and not break—any oath or promise we make before Him, walking in integrity and in the fear of the LORD.

The Fourth Commandment

> Remember the Sabbath day by keeping it holy. Six days you shall labor and do all your work, but the seventh day is a Sabbath to the LORD your God. On it you shall not do any work, neither you, nor your son or daughter, nor your manservant or maidservant, nor your animals, nor the alien within your gates. For in six days the LORD made the heavens and the earth, the sea, and all that is in them, but he rested on the seventh day. Therefore the LORD blessed the Sabbath day and made it holy. (Ex. 20:8–11)

Perspective—Our Rest in God. There is much confusion regarding the fourth commandment in the church today. Many people believe it has been repealed. That is simply untrue. The Lord's Day is part of the moral law, and is to be a delight (Isa. 58:13–14), a day that prepares us wonderfully for the six days of work that lie ahead. I believe that its central focus is upon God's sovereignty over our time, our resources, and, indeed, our very lives. God calls us to rest in Him, to find our satisfaction, security, and source in Christ alone.

Prohibitions. Like the Israelites who gathered manna in the wilderness, we are to cease from our work and worldly endeavors and trust God to provide for our needs and to renovate and to revive us.

Requirements. Notice that we are commanded to work six days of the seven. We are warned often in Scripture of the sluggard who will not work. We are to "remember" what God did for us in creation on the Lord's Day and—more importantly—what He did for us in re-creation, when Jesus rose from the tomb to make us new creatures in Christ. We gather for worship on the Lord's Day and praise Him for His Providence and wonderful grace. I commend your further study of this commandment so that you will delight in the Lord's Day too.

STUDY QUESTIONS AND EXERCISES

1. In your own words, write down a weakness or weaknesses in your own life of which you have been convicted in the preceding discussion of each of the first four of the Ten Commandments:

   a. First Commandment:

b. Second Commandment:

c. Third Commandment:

d. Fourth Commandment:

2. In Psalm 115:2–8 the nations break which of these commandments? What kinds of things are worshipped or trusted in our world today? List as many as you can think of. Is there anything inherently wrong with most of the things on your list? What is it that makes one's trust in them wrong?

3. What does Romans 1:25 tell us about the one thing all idols share?

4. Which of the first four commandments is foreseen in Genesis 2:2–3? What force do these verses give the commandment as spoken to Moses in Exodus 20?

5. Acts 20:7 speaks of the disciples' meeting together to break bread. Why was the day of rest and worship moved by the early Christians from the seventh to the first day of the week? (See Mark 16:9 and John 20:19 for some clues.)

6. In Mark 2:27, Jesus states, "The Sabbath was made for man and not man for the Sabbath." What do you suppose He meant by this? How does Isaiah 58:13–14 shed light on this question? What does Isaiah tell us are the results of delighting in God's special day?

7. While it is interesting that Jesus never mentions specifically commandments 1–4 of the Decalogue, He does say to anyone who would be His disciple, "Come, follow me" (Matt. 19:21, for instance). What is Jesus saying about His godhood and lordship when He makes such a command of His disciples? How does His statement then relate to the first four commandments?

More Verses to Ponder
Exodus 16:5, 23–30; Psalm 92:1–15; Isaiah 56:2–7; 1 Corinthians 16:2; Revelation 1:10

A Verse to Memorize
"Love the LORD your God with all your heart and with all your soul and with all your strength." (Deut. 6:5)

My Personal Action Plan to Worship and Serve God Alone

1.

2.

3.

4.

Chapter 3

The Ten Commandments (2):
Commandments 5–10

In this chapter, the Decalogue moves from dealing with our direct relationship to God, to our indirect relationship to God through our direct relationships with other people. There's a surprise waiting at command number ten, however, that should emphasize to us that the Decalogue is a single unit. All ten of the commandments ultimately deal with our relationship to our Creator God.

The Fifth Commandment

> Honor your father and your mother, so that you may live long in the land the LORD your God is giving you. (Ex. 20:12)

Perspective—Our Submission to God's Rule. This is a transitional commandment where the focus begins to shift from our duty to God to our duty to our fellow man. Of course, the focus never really shifts from God, because all sin is ultimately against God. The command focuses narrowly on the submission of children to their parents. But in a wider sense, it speaks of our submission to all earthly authority. Paul says in Romans 13:1 that, "Everyone must submit himself to the governing authorities, for there is no authority except that which God has established." Those authorities exist in the home, the school, the office or place of work, the church, and the civil government.

Prohibitions. We must avoid any behavior or speech that dishonors those in authority over us. We must not partake in rebellion against their commands or disrespect their position. Those in authority must not mistreat or provoke those under them. Nor should they require obedience to any law that opposes the clear teaching of Scripture.

Requirements. We are to see those in authority over us as extensions of God's rule over His creation. We are to pray for them and willingly submit to their commands and counsel. We are to pay taxes to the civil authority for the general welfare of society and obey rightly ordained laws. We must treat all men with the dignity and value God has attributed to them as His image bearers.

The Sixth Commandment

You shall not murder. (Ex. 20:13)

Perspective—Our Respect for Life. God is the Creator, Sustainer, and Redeemer of life (Heb. 1:1–3). Only God can take a life. We need His authorization, but that authority to bear the sword has been given only to the state, not to individuals. God instituted the death penalty in murder cases not primarily as a deterrent, although it is that, but because "in the image of God has God made man" (Gen. 9:6).

In today's world, the murder of the innocent unborn goes on unabated, while cold-blooded murderers remain alive. As mentioned earlier, Jesus elevated anger against one's brother as a form of murder. Today, anger is a plague, as the divorce rate zooms and worship of the almighty buck drives people to hate their competitors.

Prohibitions. Any action that endangers the life of another is to be avoided. Suicide, or self-murder, is a gross sin against the Creator. Anger stemming from pride, greed, and the like is an offense to God. Slaying another's character by gossip and innuendo is tantamount to murder. These things are to be shunned.

Requirements. Jesus calls us to "love your enemies and pray for those who persecute you" (Matt. 5:44). Anger and contentiousness kill relationships. But love strengthens and builds up. We need to understand that all wrongful anger is anger against God, who sustains all things by His powerful hand, and who is in absolute control of this universe.

God calls us to lives of peace and unity. This is particularly important in the church. Sins such as pride and anger separate us from other Christians, while love brings reconciliation and unity.

The Seventh Commandment

You shall not commit adultery. (Ex. 20:14)

Perspective—Our Respect for Sexual Purity. Throughout the Bible, the covenant of marriage is likened to the covenant between God and His people. Paul says in Ephesians 5:32, "[The marriage bond] is a profound mystery—but I am talking about Christ and the church." The family was the first human institution ordained by God, and it is still the foundation of society. Any thought, speech, or action that is sexually impure is in opposition to the will of God for the maintenance of the family and ultimately, for all of human society. Today, men and women are thumbing their noses at God in sexual impurity and lust, and the family is suffering the consequences.

Prohibitions. Listen to the words of the Westminster Larger Catechism (Question 139): "The sins forbidden in the seventh commandment . . . are, adultery, fornication, rape, incest, sodomy, and all unnatural lusts; all unclean imaginations, thoughts, purposes, and affections; all corrupt or filthy communications, or listening thereunto; wanton looks, . . . immodest apparel, . . . [bigamy], unjust divorce, . . . unchaste company, lascivious songs, books, pictures, [etc.]."

Requirements. God wants His people to be chaste in mind, in body, in speech, and in all our actions. Job made a pact with his eyes not to look lustfully upon a woman (Job 31:1). Job should be our example, whether male or female. Conversely, we who are married must give our bodies willingly to our mates. Let us hide in our hearts the biblical injunctions against adultery. For instance, the Proverbs conclude of the adulteress, "Her house is a highway to the grave, leading down to the chambers of death" (Prov. 7:27; see also 5:5, 23; 6:26, 32).

The Eighth Commandment

You shall not steal. (Ex. 20:15)

Perspective—Our Respect for Human Rights. Just as murder is theft of life or reputation, and adultery is theft of the sanctity of the marriage covenant, so stealing of property is the theft of one's human rights. If I steal a man's money or property, I have taken his freedom and his self-respect as well.

Interestingly, this commandment lays a foundation for private property rights, a concept rejected by godless Communism. In America, property rights have always been recognized as a basic human right.

Prohibitions. We must not take for ourselves anything that belongs to our neighbor. That includes his time, his reputation, his spouse, his money or property, his rights as a citizen and person made in the image of God. In our labor, we must not steal from our employer by being slack in our work. In business affairs, our scales and measures must be accurate, our word our bond, and all our contracts inviolable. We must avoid lawsuits, fraud, or any means of making ourselves rich at the expense of our neighbor.

Requirements. Christ would have us treat all people as we would have them treat us. Stealing is a manifestation of covetousness and a lack of contentment with what God has provided. Therefore, like Paul we ought to say, "I have learned to be content whatever the circumstances" (Phil. 4:11). We should always be fair and equitable, knowing that it is our God "who richly provides us with everything for our enjoyment" (1 Tim. 6:17). The tenth commandment also has much to say about our contentment with God's provision for us.

The Ninth Commandment

> You shall not give false testimony against your neighbor. (Ex. 20:16)

Perspective—Our Respect for Truth. Just as respect for human life, sexuality, and rights has degenerated in our society, so has the respect for truth. In our postmodern world, many people are saying that there is no truth. Everything is "relative." Ironically, the only absolute truth for the relativist is that there is no truth. But Christ said, "I am the way and the truth and the life" (John 14:6), and "[God's] word is truth" (John 17:17).

If there is no truth, then our faith and hope in Christ is in vain. We of all people must respect truth, for our God is the God of truth. We must stand up for the truth in this lost generation, speaking it, defending it, and living it. Sin, for the Christian, is "false testimony" about the saving power of the blood of Christ.

Prohibitions. As the commandment says, we are not to testify falsely against our neighbor in a court of law, or under any circumstance. But the commandment also prohibits telling lies in any event, except perhaps to save lives in time of war. We are not to call evil good or good evil (Isa. 5:20); nor are we to hide the truth where its disclosure is just. Gossip, slander, and backbiting are also forbidden, as is boasting, flattery, breach of promise, and thinking too highly of ourselves.

Requirements. We are to promote the truth in every circumstance. If our neighbor has been slandered, we need to defend his honor. We should track down gossip to its source and destroy its power. We need to report falsehood where we find it, seeking the truth in all our dealings. Finally, we need to lovingly give out the true gospel of Jesus Christ to every creature, teaching them to obey Christ in all things (Matt. 28:19–20).

The Tenth Commandment

> You shall not covet your neighbor's house. You shall not covet your neighbor's wife, or his manservant or maidservant, his ox or donkey, or anything that belongs to your neighbor. (Ex. 20:17)

Perspective—Our Respect for God. This perspective may seem strange to you, but let me explain. Covetousness is a sin of the mind. Paul said that he would not have known what coveting is if God's law had made it clear to him (Rom. 7:7). It is a mindset that envies one's neighbor and seeks its reward in the audience of this world. For example, one reason many people seek big, expensive houses and automobiles is in order to impress others with their wealth, property, and position. They want to elevate themselves in their neighbor's eyes. Covetousness rests on overweening pride.

The Christian scholar and lecturer Os Guinness has the solution to covetousness. He says that we are to live life for "The Audience of One"—the Lord God. We are to covet only His praise and His gifts, and not those of the world. Christ did not elevate Himself, but humbled Himself. Should we do otherwise?

All sin flows from breaking this commandment. When we respect the world and its ways more than we respect God, we sin.

Prohibitions. We are not to seek our dignity and value from the praise of sinful humans, but from knowing a gracious God and obeying His commandments. We are not to trust the world for our provision, but God alone.

Requirements. "Love the LORD your God with all your heart and with all your soul and with all your strength" (Deut. 6:5). Hear Christ. Follow Him and keep His commandments. Like Paul, be able to say, "I have learned to be content whatever the circumstances" (Phil. 4:11).

STUDY QUESTIONS AND EXERCISES

1. In your own words, write down a weakness, or weaknesses, in your own life of which you have been convicted in the preceding discussion of each of the last six of the Ten Commandments:

   a. Fifth Commandment:

   b. Sixth Commandment:

   c. Seventh Commandment:

   d. Eighth Commandment:

   e. Ninth Commandment:

   f. Tenth Commandment:

2. Read Luke 18:18–29. What does the ruler ask Jesus? In His initial response, what does Jesus say about humanity's condition?

    a. Which of the Ten Commandments does Jesus then quote? Do you think the man had really kept them, in light of Jesus' teaching?

    b. Which command had the ruler really neglected? Which did the ruler treasure more: his wealth or the kingdom of God? What was Jesus' reply to the people's question? How can anyone be saved?

3. The book of Proverbs has much to say about our day-to-day relationships with others, and of putting the Ten Commandments in shoe-leather. Find these proverbs and match them to the particular commandment (of the last six) to which each points.

Proverb	Commandment	Proverb	Commandment
25:18	_____	15:27	_____
29:2	_____	20:20	_____
19:16	_____	22:14	_____
16:11	_____	20:10	_____
5:15–20	_____	12:18	_____
26:11	_____	11:26	_____

4. Covetousness is a sin that shows up often in Scripture. What characters in the Bible were guilty of this sin as portrayed in the following verses?

   Genesis 3:6

   Genesis 27:6–29

   1 Samuel 2:13–17

   1 Samuel 8:3

   1 Kings 21:2–16

   Matthew 21:12–13

   Matthew 26:15–16

   Acts 8:18–23

5. Read Jeremiah 7:9–11. The Lord accused Israel of breaking several commandments. How many commandments do you see mentioned in these verses? What occasion in the New Testament do these verses remind you of?

More Verses to Ponder
Matthew 15:4–6; 2 Corinthians 8:21; James 2:11; 1 John 3:15; 1 Peter 2:12

A Verse to Memorize
"'Love the Lord your God with all your heart and with all your soul and with all your mind and with all your strength.'

The second is this: 'Love your neighbor as yourself.' There is no commandment greater than these." (Mark 12:30–31)

My Personal Action Plan to Love My Neighbor as Myself

1.

2.

3.

4.

The Christian Calling

God always has a reason for what He does. When He called us to Christ, He had a purpose in mind. Of course, God's overarching purpose is His own glory. But how are we as children of God to glorify our heavenly Father?

In this chapter, we will examine God's plan for us to bring glory to His name. It is also His plan to bring us joy that is unfathomable to the world, joy that the world will never know from its system of sin and rebellion. How do we glorify God? First, in our obedience to His commands, and second, in our discipleship to Christ.

A Call to Obedience

In recent years, a heated disagreement has raged in some evangelical circles, popularly called "the lordship debate." I must admit that I have not read extensively on either side of the issue. I suppose that's because I have always considered the answer to be obvious. As you read the verses that follow, I think you will easily see what I mean. Christians are called to obey Jesus Christ as Lord. Period.

Christians are saved by grace alone, through faith alone, in Christ's finished work alone. That is not the issue. All sides agree on that. The question seems to be whether a person can be saved and yet not want to obey Christ. Suppose a person goes forward in a revival meeting or following a gospel message and professes Christ as Savior. A few days later no change has occurred in his outward behavior, and he returns to his old life. Was such a person saved? I cannot believe that he was. Christians aren't perfectly obedient, but they want to obey, and that makes a difference in how they live.

When I was a child, I "received Christ" during vacation Bible school and was baptized. From that day until I was 33 years old, I lived a typical pagan lifestyle. I could not have cared less about what Christ had to say. Was I saved? No, not until I was 33. Then the Holy Spirit made such an impact upon my life and conscience that I was immediately convicted of certain sins. Over the intervening years, I have tried to obey Him, while clinging only to God's grace.

Dr. J. Vernon McGee used to say that he believed in the security of believers, but in the insecurity of make-believers. Don't be a make-believer, a hypocrite. Christ calls us to be His disciples. If we truly love Him, we will seriously undertake to do as our Lord commands.

Matthew 9:9

As Jesus went on from there, he saw a man named Matthew sitting at the tax collector's booth. "Follow me," he told him, and Matthew got up and followed him.

Matthew 12:49–50

Pointing to his disciples, he said, "Here are my mother and my brothers. For whoever does the will of my Father in heaven is my brother and sister and mother."

Matthew 22:36–40

"Teacher, which is the greatest commandment in the Law?"

Jesus replied, "'Love the Lord your God with all your heart and with all your soul and with all your mind.' This is the first and greatest commandment. And the second is like it: 'Love your neighbor as yourself.' All the Law and the Prophets hang on these two commandments."

Luke 8:19–21

Now Jesus' mother and brothers came to see him, but they were not able to get near him because of the crowd. Someone told him, "Your mother and brothers are standing outside, wanting to see you."

He replied, "My mother and brothers are those who hear God's word and put it into practice."

Luke 11:27–28

As Jesus was saying these things, a woman in the crowd called out, "Blessed is the mother who gave you birth and nursed you."

He replied, "Blessed rather are those who hear the word of God and obey it."

John 14:15

[Jesus said,] "If you love me, you will obey what I command."

John 14:21a

"Whoever has my commands and obeys them, he is the one who loves me."

John 14:22–24a

Then Judas (not Judas Iscariot) said, "But, Lord, why do you intend to show yourself to us and not to the world?"

Jesus replied, "If anyone loves me, he will obey my teaching. My Father will love him and we will come to him and make our home with him. He who does not love me will not obey my teaching."

John 15:10

"If you obey my commands, you will remain in my love, just as I have obeyed my Father's commands and remain in his love."

John 15:14

"You are my friends if you do what I command."

1 Corinthians 7:19b

Keeping God's commands is what counts.

Ephesians 5:10

. . . find out what pleases the Lord.

Philippians 1:27a

Whatever happens, conduct yourselves in a manner worthy of the gospel of Christ.

Philippians 4:9

Whatever you have learned or received or heard from me, or seen in me—put it into practice. And the God of peace will be with you.

1 Thessalonians 4:1–2

Finally, brothers, we instructed you how to live in order to please God, as in fact you are living. Now we ask you and urge you in the Lord Jesus to do this more and more. For you know what instructions we gave you by the authority of the Lord Jesus.

2 Thessalonians 3:13

As for you, brothers, never tire of doing what is right.

1 John 2:3–6

We know that we have come to know him if we obey his commands. The man who says, "I know him," but does not do what he commands is a liar, and the truth is not in him. But if anyone obeys his word, God's love is truly made complete in him. This is how we know we are in him: Whoever claims to live in him must walk as Jesus did.

1 John 3:21–22
> Dear friends, if our hearts do not condemn us, we have confidence before God and receive from him anything we ask, because we obey his commands and do what pleases him.

1 John 5:3a
> This is love for God: to obey his commands.

STUDY QUESTIONS AND EXERCISES

1. After reading all the preceding verses in this chapter, what do you believe they are teaching us about Christ's position as Lord, and our obligation to obey Him?

2. Read Matthew 6:24. How many different "Lords" can anyone serve? Why? To which of the Ten Commandments does that verse directly relate? Where are you looking for applause: from people or from God?

3. Ezra was a child of God, a man on whom was "the good hand of God." Read Ezra 7:10. Why was the Lord with him?

4. Read 2 Chronicles 31:20–21. King Hezekiah was a prosperous servant of God. Why? List all the reasons these verses give for his prosperity.

5. Read the first chapter of Proverbs. Why did Solomon write the book of Proverbs? What are the results of rejecting its wisdom?

6. Do you share my experience as related at the opening of this chapter? Many do. What are your thoughts about that experience?

More Verses to Ponder
Exodus 19:5; Psalm 111:10; Proverbs 19:16; Acts 5:29

A Verse to Memorize
"Whoever has my [Jesus'] commands and obeys them, he is the one who loves me." (John 14:21)

My Personal Action Plan to Obey Christ

1.

2.

3.

4.

A CALL TO SERVICE AND DISCIPLESHIP

Jesus said in the Great Commission of Matthew 28:18–20, "All authority in heaven and on earth has been given to me. Therefore go and make disciples of all nations, baptizing them in the name of the Father and of the Son and of the Holy Spirit, and teaching them to obey everything I have commanded you. And surely I am with you always, to the very end of the age."

What is a disciple? A disciple is a follower of Christ, one who has left all to follow Him. John Broadus, in his 1886 commentary on the gospel of Matthew, said this: "To disciple a person to Christ is to bring him into the relation of pupil to teacher, 'taking his yoke' of authoritative instruction (11:29), accepting what he says as true because he says it, and submitting to his requirements as right because he makes them." Just to say "I'm a Christian," doesn't make it so. Jesus came to call disciples. Taking Christ's "yoke" is all-important.

Christian discipleship involves a general call to obedience, as we saw in chapter 1. But it is also a general call by Christ to servanthood. Christ "did not come to be served, but to serve . . ." (Matt. 20:28). That involves humility (chap. 6), and the willingness to deny oneself for the benefit of others. Jesus said in Matthew 10:24, "A student [disciple] is not above his teacher, nor a servant above his master." In other words, if Christ humbled Himself and served others, can we do otherwise?

As you study these verses, ask yourself, "Given my gifts, calling, and circumstances, how am I best qualified to serve others?" Then chart a course of action and follow Christ who says, "My yoke is easy and my burden is light" (Matt. 11:30).

Matthew 20:26b–28
"Instead, whoever wants to become great among you must be your servant, and whoever wants to be first must be your slave—just as the Son of Man did not come to be served, but to serve, and to give his life as a ransom for many." [Cf. Mark 10:43–45; Luke 2:26–27.]

Mark 9:35
Sitting down, Jesus called to the Twelve and said, "If anyone wants to be first, he must be the very last, and the servant of all."

Luke 9:23
Then he said to [His disciples]: "If anyone would come after me, he must deny himself and take up his cross daily and follow me."

Luke 12:35

"Be dressed ready for service and keep your lamps burning."

Luke 14:12–14

Then Jesus said to his host, "When you give a luncheon or dinner, do not invite your friends, your brothers or relatives, or your rich neighbors; if you do, they may invite you back and so you will be repaid. But when you give a banquet, invite the poor, the crippled, the lame, the blind, and you will be blessed. Although they cannot repay you, you will be repaid at the resurrection of the righteous."

Luke 14:25–33

Large crowds were traveling with Jesus, and turning to them he said: "If anyone comes to me and does not hate his father and mother, his wife and children, his brothers and sisters—yes, even his own life—he cannot be my disciple. And anyone who does not carry his cross and follow me cannot be my disciple.

"Suppose one of you wants to build a tower. Will he not first sit down and estimate the cost to see if he has enough money to complete it? For if he lays the foundation and is not able to finish it, everyone who sees it will ridicule him, saying, 'This fellow began to build and was not able to finish.'

"Or suppose a king is about to go to war against another king. Will he not first sit down and consider whether he is able with ten thousand men to oppose the one coming against him with twenty thousand? If he is not able, he will send a delegation while the other is still a long way off and will ask for terms of peace. In the same way, any of you who does not give up everything he has cannot be my disciple."

John 13:13–17

[After washing his disciples' feet, Jesus said,] "You call me 'Teacher' and 'Lord,' and rightly so, for that is what I am. Now that I, your Lord and Teacher, have washed your feet, you also should wash one another's feet. I have set you an example that you should do as I have done for you. I tell you the truth, no servant is greater than his master, nor is a messenger greater than the one who sent him. Now that you know these things, you will be blessed if you do them."

Romans 12:1–2

Therefore, I urge you, brothers, in view of God's mercy, to offer your bodies as living sacrifices, holy and pleasing to God—this is your spiritual act of worship. Do not conform any longer to the pattern of this world, but be transformed by the renewing of your mind. Then you will be able to test and approve what God's will is—his good, pleasing and perfect will.

Romans 12:11–13

Never be lacking in zeal, but keep your spiritual fervor, serving the Lord. Be joyful in hope, patient in affliction, faithful in prayer. Share with God's people who are in need. Practice hospitality.

Romans 15:1–3a

We who are strong ought to bear with the failings of the weak and not to please ourselves. Each of us should please his neighbor for his good, to build him up. For even Christ did not please himself. . . .

1 Corinthians 10:24

Nobody should seek his own good, but the good of others.

2 Corinthians 5:9–10

So we make it our goal to please [Christ], whether we are at home in the body or away from it. For we must all appear before the judgment seat of Christ, that each one may receive what is due him for the things done while in the body, whether good or bad.

2 Corinthians 5:14–15

For Christ's love compels us, because we are convinced that one died for all, and therefore all died. And he died for all, that those who live should no longer live for themselves but for him who died for them and was raised again.

2 Corinthians 9:6–7

Remember this: Whoever sows sparingly will also reap sparingly, and whoever sows generously will also reap generously. Each man should give what he has decided in his heart to give, not reluctantly or under compulsion, for God loves a cheerful giver.

Galatians 6:1–2

Brothers, if someone is caught in a sin, you who are spiritual should restore him gently. But watch yourself, or you also may be tempted. Carry each other's burdens, and in this way you will fulfill the law of Christ.

Galatians 6:9–10

Let us not become weary in doing good, for at the proper time we will reap a harvest if we do not give up. Therefore, as we have opportunity, let us do good to all people, especially to those who belong to the family of believers.

Philippians 2:3–8

Do nothing out of selfish ambition or vain conceit, but in humility consider others better than yourselves. Each of you should look not only to your own interests, but also to the interests of others.

Your attitude should be the same as that of Christ Jesus:

Who, being in very nature God,
    did not consider equality with God something to be
        grasped,
but made himself nothing,

taking the very likeness of a servant,
being made in human likeness.
And being found in appearance as a man,
he humbled himself
and became obedient to death—
even death on a cross!

Hebrews 6:10–12

God is not unjust; he will not forget your work and the love you have shown him as you have helped his people and continue to help them. We want each one of you to show this same diligence to the very end, in order to make your hope sure. We do not want you to become lazy, but to imitate those who through faith and patience inherit what has been promised.

Hebrews 10:24–25

And let us consider how we may spur one another on toward love and good deeds. Let us not give up meeting together, as some are in the habit of doing, but let us encourage one another—and all the more as you see the Day approaching.

Hebrews 12:1–3

Therefore, since we are surrounded by such a great cloud of witnesses, let us throw off everything that hinders and the sin that so easily entangles, and let us run with perseverance the race marked out for us. Let us fix our eyes on Jesus, the author and perfecter of our faith, who for the joy set before him endured the cross, scorning its shame, and sat down at the right hand of the throne of God. Consider him who endured such opposition from sinful men, so that you will not grow weary and lose heart.

Hebrews 13:1–3

Keep on loving each other as brothers. Do not forget to entertain strangers, for by so doing some people have entertained angels without knowing it. Remember those in prison as if you were their fellow prisoners, and those who are mistreated as if you yourselves were suffering.

Hebrews 13:13

Let us, then, go to him outside the camp, bearing the disgrace he bore.

Hebrews 13:16

And do not forget to do good and to share with others, for with such sacrifices God is pleased.

James 1:27

Religion that God our Father accepts as pure and faultless is this: to look after orphans and widows in their distress and to keep oneself from being polluted by the world.

1 Peter 4:9–10

Offer hospitality to one another without grumbling. Each one should use whatever gift he has received to serve others, faithfully administering God's grace in its various forms.

2 Peter 1:5–11

For this very reason, make every effort to add to your faith goodness; and to goodness, knowledge; and to knowledge, self-control; and to self-control, perseverance; and to perseverance, godliness; and to godliness, brotherly kindness; and to brotherly kindness, love. For if you possess these qualities in increasing measure, they will keep you from being ineffective and unproductive in your knowledge of our Lord Jesus Christ. But if anyone does not have them, he is nearsighted and blind, and has forgotten that he has been cleansed from his past sins.

Therefore, my brothers, be all the more eager to make your calling and election sure. For if you do these things, you will never fall, and you will receive a rich welcome into the eternal kingdom of our Lord and Savior Jesus Christ.

2 Peter 3:14

So then, dear friends, since you are looking forward to [His return], make every effort to be found spotless, blameless and at peace with him.

STUDY QUESTIONS AND EXERCISES

1. Read Deuteronomy 15:7–15. What is God's command to the Israelites regarding the poor among them? What was God's promise to those who obeyed? Does God intend to stamp out poverty (v. 11)? Why do you think He allows people to be poor? What rules were to be followed when releasing slaves? Why?

2. In Matthew 25:32–45, Jesus tells of the separation of the "sheep from the goats" at the final judgment. What does Jesus tell us will be characteristic of each group? What comparison did Jesus make between His brothers and Himself in verse 40?

3. Read Luke 10:25–37, the parable of the "Good Samaritan." Who may we assume "our neighbors" are from Jesus' teaching? Do you see yourself in this parable? Are you the wounded man? The thief? The priest or Levite? Or are you the Samaritan? Which does Christ tell us to emulate?

4. Read John 13:1–14. What is going on in these verses? Why do you suppose Peter objected? What lesson do these verses have for us today? How do they teach the way of servanthood?

5. In Luke 9:23 Jesus speaks of a follower taking up his "cross." What does He mean by that? What is our "cross"? Are our crosses all the same, or do we Christians each bear a different cross? How does your cross relate to servanthood?

More Verses to Ponder

Proverbs 17:2; Isaiah 58:6–7; 1 Corinthians 9:18–22; 2 Corinthians 4:5; 8:9

A Verse to Memorize

"If anyone would come after me, he must deny himself and take up his cross daily and follow me." (Luke 9:23)

My Personal Action Plan to Follow Christ in Servanthood

1.

2.

3.

4.

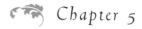

Chapter 5

The Christian Life

If God's calling for the Christian is to obedience and servanthood, what then are to be the chief defining characteristics of the Christian life? That question is partially answered
in this chapter: "Love, Unity, and Kindness," and "Faith and
Life in the Spirit." We'll take up other marks of Christian
character such as humility and holiness in later chapters. But
first and foremost, we Christians are called to live supernatural, Spirit-filled lives. Without the Spirit of God living in us
by faith, we cannot love others as we ought, unity is fragile at
best, our acts of kindness may be cruel (Prov. 12:10), our humility would vanish in pride, and our holiness would be
nonexistent.

LOVE, UNITY, AND KINDNESS

If we were to boil all of the commands of the Bible down to
one short rule it would be, "Love God and love your neighbor"
(see Mark 12:30–31). Paul says in Romans 13:8–10,

> Let no debt remain outstanding, except the continuing
> debt to love one another, for he who loves his fellow-
> man has fulfilled the law. The commandments, "Do not
> commit adultery," "Do not murder," "Do not steal,"

"Do not covet," and whatever other commandment
there may be, are summed up in this one rule: "Love
your neighbor as yourself." Love does no harm to its
neighbor. Therefore love is the fulfillment of the law.

That is why this topic has been placed near the top, after
"A Call to Obedience" and "Christian Service and Discipleship." All of the other topics show how we carry out the command to love God and our neighbor day by day.

But love, unity, and kindness to others is not a topic that
bursts upon the scene in the New Testament. The Scriptures of
the Old Testament are filled with it. It could not be otherwise,
for "God is love" (1 John 4:8). Love is a defining characteristic
of our Lord.

Way back in Leviticus 19:18 we read God's command,
"Love your neighbor as yourself." In Proverbs 10:12 we see love
contrasted with hate. "Hatred stirs up dissension, but love covers over all wrongs." And the psalmist sings of, "How good and
pleasant it is when brothers live together in unity!" (Ps. 133:1.)
Unity among brothers is the product of *agape* love between
them. It is a love that is wonderfully defined for us in 1
Corinthians 13.

As you study and discuss the following commandments, try
to see two things: First, try to understand how love is to be
manifested in our daily lives. Then list all the benefits of a loving lifestyle, for your family, your church, and your community.

Matthew 7:12

"In everything, do to others what you would have them do
to you, for this sums up the Law and the Prophets." [Cf.
Mark 12:31; Luke 10:27.]

Luke 6:27–36

"But I tell you who hear me: Love your enemies, do good to
those who hate you, bless those who curse you, pray for
those who mistreat you. If someone strikes you on one

cheek, turn to him the other also. If someone takes your cloak, do not stop him from taking your tunic. Give to everyone who asks you, and if anyone takes what belongs to you, do not demand it back. Do to others as you would have them do to you.

"If you love those who love you, what credit is that to you? Even 'sinners' love those who love them. And if you do good to those who do good to you, what credit is that to you? Even 'sinners' do that. And if you lend to those from whom you expect repayment, what credit is that to you? Even 'sinners' lend to 'sinners,' expecting to be repaid in full. But love your enemies, do good to them, and lend to them without expecting to get anything back. Then your reward will be great, and you will be sons of the Most High, because he is kind to the ungrateful and wicked. Be merciful, just as your Father is merciful." [Cf. Matt. 5:38–48.]

John 13:34–35

"A new command I give you: Love one another. As I have loved you, so you must love one another. By this all men will know that you are my disciples, if you love one another."

John 15:12–13

"My command is this: Love each other as I have loved you. Greater love has no one than this, that he lay down his life for his friends."

John 15:17

"This is my command: Love each other."

Romans 12:9–10, 13–18

Love must be sincere. Hate what is evil; cling to what is good. Be devoted to one another in brotherly love. Honor one another above yourselves. . . . Share with God's people who are in need. Practice hospitality.

Bless those who persecute you; bless and do not curse. Rejoice with those who rejoice; mourn with those who mourn. Live in harmony with one another. Do not be proud, but be willing to associate with people of low position. Do not be conceited.

Do not repay anyone evil for evil. Be careful to do what is right in the eyes of everybody. If it is possible, as far as it depends on you, live at peace with everyone.

Romans 13:8–10

Let no debt remain outstanding, except the continuing debt to love one another, for he who loves his fellow man has fulfilled the law. The commandments, "Do not commit adultery," "Do not murder," "Do not steal," "Do not covet," and whatever other commandment there may be, are summed up in this one rule: "Love your neighbor as yourself." Love does no harm to its neighbor. Therefore love is the fulfillment of the law.

Romans 14:13

Therefore let us stop passing judgment on one another. Instead, make up your mind not to put any stumbling block or obstacle in your brother's way.

1 Corinthians 10:32–11:1

Do not cause anyone to stumble, whether Jews, Greeks or the church of God—even as I try to please everybody in every way. For I am not seeking my own good but the good of many, so that they may be saved. Follow my example as I follow the example of Christ. [Cf. 1 Cor. 13 for a treatise from Paul on love.]

1 Corinthians 14:1a

Follow the way of love. . . .

1 Corinthians 16:14

Do everything in love.

Galatians 5:13–14

You, my brothers, were called to be free. But do not use your freedom to indulge the sinful nature; rather serve one another in love. The entire law is summed up in a single command: "Love your neighbor as yourself."

Galatians 6:10

Therefore, as we have opportunity, let us do good to all people, especially to those who belong to the family of believers.

Ephesians 4:1–3

As a prisoner for the Lord, then, I urge you to live a life worthy of the calling you have received. Be completely humble and gentle; be patient, bearing with one another in love. Make every effort to keep the unity of the Spirit through the bond of peace.

Ephesians 4:32

Be kind and compassionate to one another, forgiving each other, just as in Christ God forgave you.

Ephesians 5:1–2

Be imitators of God, therefore, as dearly loved children and live a life of love, just as Christ loved us and gave himself up for us as a fragrant offering and sacrifice to God.

Philippians 4:5

Let your gentleness be evident to all. The Lord is near.

Colossians 3:12–14

Therefore, as God's chosen people, holy and dearly loved, clothe yourselves with compassion, kindness, humility, gentleness and patience. Bear with each other and forgive whatever grievances you may have against one another. Forgive as the Lord forgave you. And over all these virtues put on love, which binds them all together in perfect unity.

1 Thessalonians 4:9–10

Now about brotherly love we do not need to write to you, for you yourselves have been taught by God to love each other. And in fact, you do love all the brothers throughout Macedonia. Yet we urge you, brothers, to do so more and more.

1 Thessalonians 5:15

Make sure that nobody pays back wrong for wrong, but always try to be kind to each other and to everyone else.

1 Timothy 6:11

But you, man of God, flee from all of this [love of money], and pursue righteousness, godliness, faith, love, endurance and gentleness.

2 Timothy 2:22

Flee the evil desires of youth, and pursue righteousness, faith, love and peace, along with those who call on the Lord out of a pure heart.

2 Timothy 2:24

And the Lord's servant must not quarrel; instead, he must be kind to everyone, able to teach, not resentful.

Hebrews 13:1

Keep on loving each other as brothers.

James 2:8–11

If you really keep the royal law found in Scripture, "Love your neighbor as yourself," you are doing right. But if you show favoritism, you sin and are convicted by the law as lawbreakers. For whoever keeps the whole law and yet stumbles at just one point is guilty of breaking all of it. For he who said, "Do not commit adultery," also said, "Do not murder."

If you do not commit adultery but do commit murder, you
have become a lawbreaker.

1 Peter 1:22
Now that you have purified yourselves by obeying the truth
so that you have sincere love for your brothers, love one another deeply, from the heart.

1 Peter 3:8–9
Finally, all of you, live in harmony with one another; be sympathetic, love as brothers, be compassionate and humble.
Do not repay evil with evil or insult with insult, but with
blessing, because to this you were called so that you may inherit a blessing.

1 Peter 4:8
Above all, love each other deeply, because love covers over a
multitude of sins.

2 Peter 1:5–7
For this very reason, make every effort to add to your faith
goodness; and to goodness, knowledge; and to knowledge,
self-control; and to self-control, perseverance; and to perseverance, godliness; and to godliness, brotherly kindness;
and to brotherly kindness, love.

1 John 3:11–18
This is the message you heard from the beginning: We should
love one another. Do not be like Cain, who belonged to the
evil one and murdered his brother. And why did he murder
him? Because his own actions were evil and his brother's were
righteous. Do not be surprised, my brothers, if the world
hates you. We know that we have passed from death to life,
because we love our brothers. Anyone who does not love remains in death. Anyone who hates his brother is a murderer,
and you know that no murderer has eternal life in him.

This is how we know what love is: Jesus Christ laid down his life for us. And we ought to lay down our lives for our brothers. If anyone has material possessions and sees his brother in need but has no pity on him, how can the love of God be in him? Dear children, let us not love with words or tongue but with actions and in truth.

2 John 5–6

And now, dear lady, I am not writing you a new command but one we have had from the beginning. I ask that we love one another. And this is love: that we walk in obedience to his commands. As you have heard from the beginning, his command is that you walk in love.

STUDY QUESTIONS AND EXERCISES

1. Read 1 Corinthians 13. In your own words, list all of the qualities of love that you can find. Why do you think love is greater than faith and hope as Paul says in verse 13?

2. First Corinthians 8:1 states that "knowledge puffs up, but love builds up." In what ways can knowledge be used harmfully? In what ways can knowledge be used to complement love between Christians?

3. Go back through the verses of this chapter. List all the specific actions we are told to take to promote love, unity, and kindness in our lives.

4. Read the story of David and Jonathan in 1 Samuel 20. How was real brotherly love exemplified in their friendship? How can we learn from them to do likewise?

5. Read the story of Naomi, Ruth, and Boaz in Ruth 1–3. How was the love of Christ exemplified in their lives? How was Leviticus 19:34 fulfilled by Naomi? By Boaz?

More Verses to Ponder
   Deuteronomy 10:19; Proverbs 15:17; 17:9, 17; Luke 10:29–37

A Verse to Memorize
   "Be kind and compassionate to one another, forgiving each other, just as in Christ God forgave you." (Eph. 4:32)

My Personal Action Plan to Seek Love, Unity, and Kindness

1.

2.

3.

4.

FAITH AND LIFE IN THE SPIRIT

   "Without faith it is impossible to please God." So says the writer to the Hebrews in 11:6. We are justified—declared to be righteous and acceptable to God—through faith, but faith does not stop there. We must also "live by faith" once we have been justified (Rom. 1:17; Hab. 2:4). What does that mean?
   Books could be written and have been written on the subject. Let's go back to Hebrews 11 to begin our brief overview. Verse 6 continues, ". . . because anyone who comes to [God]

must believe that he exists and that he rewards those who earnestly seek him."

The prevalent worldview of our society is that we live in a closed, mechanistic universe that operates only according to the laws inherent in its own system. That is called the "naturalistic" view. But the worldview of faith is "supernatural." For the man or woman of faith, the universe operates by the providence of God. He "sustain[s] all things by his powerful word" (Heb. 1:3). God has established those "natural" laws supernaturally and may alter them if He wishes, as He may do in healing someone in an extraordinary way.

We walk by faith when we worship God, when we obey His commands, when we trust in His provision for our lives, when we rest in Him, when we believe His promises, when we pray to Him expectantly, when we serve Him joyfully, when we allow Him to guide us and change us, and when we rely not on ourselves or any other creature or substance, but upon the One who created us and who has redeemed us.

As the writer to the Hebrews also says; "Let us [therefore] hold unswervingly to the hope we profess, for he who promised is faithful" (Heb. 10:23).

Mark 1:14–15

After John was put in prison, Jesus went into Galilee, proclaiming the good news of God. "The time has come," he said. "The kingdom of God is near. Repent and believe the good news!"

Mark 11:22

"Have faith in God," Jesus [said].

John 6:28–29

Then they asked him, "What must we do to do the works God requires?"

Jesus answered, "The work of God is this: to believe in the one he has sent."

John 15:4–5

"Remain in me, and I will remain in you. No branch can bear fruit by itself; it must remain in the vine. Neither can you bear fruit unless you remain in me.

"I am the vine; you are the branches. If a man remains in me and I in him, he will bear much fruit; apart from me you can do nothing."

Romans 12:11–12a

Never be lacking in zeal, but keep your spiritual fervor, serving the Lord. Be joyful in hope. . . .

Romans 14:1–3

Accept him whose faith is weak, without passing judgment on disputable matters. One man's faith allows him to eat everything, but another man, whose faith is weak, eats only vegetables. The man who eats everything must not look down on him who does not, and the man who does not eat everything must not condemn the man who does, for God has accepted him.

1 Corinthians 16:13–14

Be on your guard; stand firm in the faith; be men of courage; be strong. Do everything in love.

2 Corinthians 5:7

We live by faith, not by sight.

Galatians 5:16–26

So I say, live by the Spirit, and you will not gratify the desires of the sinful nature. For the sinful nature desires what is contrary to the Spirit, and the Spirit what is contrary to the sinful nature. They are in conflict with each other, so that you do not do what you want. But if you are led by the Spirit, you are not under law.

The acts of the sinful nature are obvious: sexual immorality, impurity and debauchery; idolatry and witchcraft; hatred, discord, jealousy, fits of rage, selfish ambition, dissensions, factions and envy; drunkenness, orgies, and the like. I warn you, as I did before, that those who live like this will not inherit the kingdom of God.

But the fruit of the Spirit is love, joy, peace, patience, kindness, goodness, faithfulness, gentleness and self-control. Against such things there is no law. Those who belong to Christ Jesus have crucified the sinful nature with its passions and desires. Since we live by the Spirit, let us keep in step with the Spirit. Let us not become conceited, provoking and envying each other.

1 Thessalonians 5:19

Do not put out the Spirit's fire.

1 Timothy 6:11–16

But you, man of God, flee from all this [greed], and pursue righteousness, godliness, faith, love, endurance and gentleness. Fight the good fight of the faith. Take hold of the eternal life to which you were called when you made your good confession in the presence of many witnesses. In the sight of God, who gives life to everything, and of Christ Jesus, who while testifying before Pontius Pilate made the good confession, I charge you to keep this command without spot or blame until the appearing of our Lord Jesus Christ, which God will bring about in his own time—God, the blessed and only Ruler, the King of kings and Lord of lords, who alone is immortal and who lives in unapproachable light, whom no one has seen or can see. To him be honor and might forever. Amen.

2 Timothy 2:22

Flee the evil desires of youth, and pursue righteousness, faith, love and peace, along with those who call on the Lord out of a pure heart.

Hebrews 3:7–8, 12–13

So, as the Holy Spirit says:

> "Today, if you hear his voice,
>   do not harden your hearts
> as you did in the rebellion,
>   during the time of testing in the desert. . . ."

See to it, brothers, that none of you has a sinful, unbelieving heart that turns away from the living God. But encourage one another daily, as long as it is called Today, so that none of you may be hardened by sin's deceitfulness.

Hebrews 4:14–16

Therefore, since we have a great high priest who has gone through the heavens, Jesus the Son of God, let us hold firmly to the faith we profess. For we do not have a high priest who is unable to sympathize with our weaknesses, but we have one who has been tempted in every way, just as we are—yet was without sin. Let us then approach the throne of grace with confidence, so that we may receive mercy and find grace to help us in our time of need.

Hebrews 10:19–23

Therefore, brothers, since we have confidence to enter the Most Holy Place by the blood of Jesus, by a new and living way opened for us through the curtain, that is, his body, and since we have a great high priest over the house of God, let us draw near to God with a sincere heart in full assurance of faith, having our hearts sprinkled to cleanse us from a guilty conscience and having our bodies washed with pure water. Let us hold unswervingly to the hope we profess, for he who promised is faithful.

James 2:14–19

What good is it, my brothers, if a man claims to have faith but has no deeds? Can such faith save him? Suppose a brother or sister is without clothes and daily food. If one of you says to him, "Go, I wish you well; keep warm and well fed," but does nothing about his physical needs, what good is it? In the same way, faith by itself, if it is not accompanied by action, is dead.

But someone will say, "You have faith; I have deeds."

Show me your faith without deeds, and I will show you my faith by what I do. You believe that there is one God. Good! Even the demons believe that—and shudder.

1 Peter 3:15a

But in your hearts set apart Christ as Lord.

1 Peter 5:8–9

Be self-controlled and alert. Your enemy the devil prowls around like a roaring lion looking for someone to devour. Resist him, standing firm in the faith, because you know that your brothers throughout the world are undergoing the same kind of sufferings.

Jude 20a

But you, dear friends, build yourselves up in your most holy faith. . . .

STUDY QUESTIONS AND EXERCISES

1. Remember the story of Joseph and his brothers, who sold him into slavery in Egypt (Gen. 37, 39–50)? In Genesis 50:19–20, Joseph spoke to his brothers who were afraid that he might take revenge. What did he tell them? How could God use their sin for good purposes? Does God still do this? What does this mean for our walk with Him?

2. In Daniel 3 we are told of three men with extraordinary faith. How did they exhibit it? What happened to them? Would you have faith like that in those circumstances?

3. Read Genesis 15:1–6. What was the promise God made? What was Abraham's response to it? What was the effect of his response? Was the promise fulfilled?

4. Read Habbakuk 3:17–19. Under what circumstances does the prophet say he will rejoice in God? Have you ever gone through similar things in your Christian life? Did you rejoice?

5. In 1 Corinthians 13:13, Paul mentions "faith, hope and love." How are faith and hope similar? How are they different?

More Verses to Ponder
Psalm 9:9–10; 34:8; Proverbs 3:5–6; 14:26; Luke 17:5

A Verse to Memorize
"I am the vine; you are the branches. If a man remains in me and I in him, he will bear much fruit; apart from me you can do nothing." (John 15:5)

My Personal Action Plan to Walk by Faith, Not by Sight

1.

2.

3.

4.

Chapter 6

The Christian Mind

If the Christian is to live a supernatural life of faith, exhibiting fruit that can only be borne by the Spirit of God, what should be the characteristics of his mind and thought life? We are told in Proverbs 4:23, "Keep thy heart with all diligence; for out of it are the issues of life" (KJV). Again, Proverbs 23:7 says, "For as [a person] thinketh in his heart, so is he" (KJV). Words and actions have their beginnings in the thoughts of our hearts. What and how we think is of extreme importance. We need the Holy Spirit's control of our thought life in order for it to be pleasing to God. That thought life will then be essentially one of prayer and thanksgiving.

PRAYER AND THANKSGIVING

Prayer is our part of the communication process between God and us. God's part is His Word made real to us by the Holy Spirit's application to our lives. God speaks through His Word to us, and we speak back in prayer and thanksgiving.

Many have wondered why prayer is necessary at all. If God has ordained all that will ever come to pass on this earth, so that nothing catches Him by surprise, then why pray for things to happen? First, because as the following verses testify, we are commanded to pray as a central endeavor of our lives. Second, more happens when we pray than just communication of needs. We are changed and God is glorified. Third, while it is true that God has foreordained all history, He also has foreordained the means through which He acts. Our prayer is a means God uses to accomplish His purposes.

One aid to prayer is the acronym, "ACTS." The letters stand for what should be four parts of our prayer life. "A" stands for "Adoration." We love God and we tell Him so in our time with Him. "C" is for "Confession." While Adoration speaks of who God is, confession speaks of our own condition as sinners. We need to confess our sins and receive God's cleansing. "T" represents "Thanksgiving." God is our security, our satisfaction, and the source of all we have. Thank God for His great benefits and glorify Him. Finally, "S" stands for "Supplication." This part of prayer asks God for his help, such as healing for loved ones. Review the "Lord's Prayer" on the next pages and identify the parts of the ACTS formula in it.

Prayer is a mark of living faith. We pray believing in our God who hears us and answers our prayer according to His infinite love.

Matthew 6:5–13

"And when you pray, do not be like the hypocrites, for they love to pray standing in the synagogues and on the street corners to be seen by men. I tell you the truth, they have received their reward in full. When you pray, go into your room, close the door and pray to your Father, who is unseen. Then your Father, who sees what is done in secret, will reward you. And when you pray, do not keep on babbling like pagans, for they think they will be heard because of their many words. Do not be like them, for your Father knows what you need before you ask him.

"This, then, is how you should pray:

'Our Father in heaven,
hallowed be your name,
your kingdom come,
your will be done
    on earth as it is in heaven.
Give us today our daily bread.
Forgive us our debts,
    as we also have forgiven our debtors.
And lead us not into temptation,
but deliver us from the evil one.'"

Matthew 7:7–11

"Ask and it will be given to you; seek and you will find; knock
and the door will be opened to you. For everyone who asks
receives; he who seeks finds; and to him who knocks, the
door will be opened.

"Which of you, if his son asks for bread, will give him a
stone? Or if he asks for a fish, will give him a snake? If you,
then, though you are evil, know how to give good gifts to
your children, how much more will your Father in heaven
give good gifts to those who ask him!"

Luke 18:1–8a

Then Jesus told his disciples a parable to show them that
they should always pray and not give up. He said: "In a certain town there was a judge who neither feared God nor
cared about men. And there was a widow in that town who
kept coming to him with the plea, 'Grant me justice against
my adversary.'

"For some time he refused. But finally he said to himself,
'Even though I don't fear God or care about men, yet because this widow keeps bothering me, I will see that she gets
justice, so that she won't eventually wear me out with her
coming!'"

And the Lord said, "Listen to what the unjust judge says.
And will not God bring about justice for his chosen ones,

who cry out to him day and night? Will he keep putting them off? I tell you, he will see that they get justice, and quickly."

Romans 12:12

Be joyful in hope, patient in affliction, faithful in prayer.

Ephesians 5:19–20

Speak to one another with psalms, hymns and spiritual songs. Sing and make music in your heart to the Lord, always giving thanks to God the Father for everything, in the name of our Lord Jesus Christ.

Ephesians 6:18

And pray in the Spirit on all occasions with all kinds of prayers and requests. With this in mind, be alert and always keep on praying for all the saints.

Philippians 3:1a

Finally, my brothers, rejoice in the Lord!

Philippians 4:4, 6–7

Rejoice in the Lord always. I will say it again: Rejoice! . . . Do not be anxious about anything, but in everything, by prayer and petition, with thanksgiving, present your requests to God. And the peace of God, which transcends all understanding, will guard your hearts and your minds in Christ Jesus.

Colossians 3:15b, 16b–17

And be thankful. . . . with gratitude in your hearts to God. And whatever you do, whether in word or deed, do it all in the name of the Lord Jesus, giving thanks to God the Father through him.

Colossians 4:2–3

Devote yourselves to prayer, being watchful and thankful. And pray for us, too, that God may open a door for our message, so that we may proclaim the mystery of Christ, for which I am in chains.

1 Thessalonians 5:16–18

Be joyful always; pray continually; give thanks in all circumstances, for this is God's will for you in Christ Jesus.

1 Timothy 2:1–8

I urge, then, first of all, that requests, prayers, intercession and thanksgiving be made for everyone—for kings and all those in authority, that we may live peaceful and quiet lives in all godliness and holiness. This is good, and pleases God our Savior, who wants all men to be saved and to come to a knowledge of the truth. For there is one God and one mediator between God and men, the man Christ Jesus, who gave himself as a ransom for all men—the testimony given in its proper time. And for this purpose I was appointed a herald and an apostle—I am telling the truth, I am not lying—and a teacher of the true faith to the Gentiles.

I want men everywhere to lift up holy hands in prayer, without anger or disputing.

Hebrews 4:14–16

Therefore, since we have a great high priest who has gone through the heavens, Jesus the Son of God, let us hold firmly to the faith we profess. For we do not have a high priest who is unable to sympathize with our weaknesses, but we have one who has been tempted in every way, just as we are—yet was without sin. Let us then approach the throne of grace with confidence, so that we may receive mercy, and find grace to help us in our time of need.

Hebrews 12:28–29

Therefore, since we are receiving a kingdom that cannot be shaken, let us be thankful, and so worship God acceptably with reverence and awe, for "our God is a consuming fire."

Hebrews 13:15

Through Jesus, therefore, let us continually offer to God a sacrifice of praise—the fruit of lips that confess his name.

James 5:13–18

Is any one of you in trouble? He should pray. Is anyone happy? Let him sing songs of praise. Is any one of you sick? He should call the elders of the church to pray over him and anoint him with oil in the name of the Lord. And the prayer offered in faith will make the sick person well; the Lord will raise him up. If he has sinned, he will be forgiven. Therefore confess your sins to each other and pray for each other so that you may be healed. The prayer of a righteous man is powerful and effective.

Elijah was a man just like us. He prayed earnestly that it would not rain, and it did not rain on the land for three and a half years. Again he prayed, and the heavens gave rain, and the earth produced its crops.

1 Peter 4:7, 13a

The end of all things is near. Therefore be clear minded and self-controlled so that you can pray. . . . rejoice that you participate in the sufferings of Christ.

Jude 20

But you, dear friends, build yourselves up in your most holy faith and pray in the Holy Spirit.

STUDY QUESTIONS AND EXERCISES

1. Sometimes, God refuses to hear and answer prayer. What do the following verses tell us about His reasons for this?

   a. Psalm 66:18.

   b. Proverbs 1:24–28; 21:13; 28:9.

c. Isaiah 1:15.

d. Micah 3:4.

e. Zechariah 7:12–13.

f. John 9:31.

g. James 1:6–7; 4:3.

h. 1 Peter 3:7.

2. Which part of our ACTS formula does each of these Old Testament people use?

a. David in Psalm 51:3–4.

b. The sailors in Jonah 1:14.

c. Moses in Exodus 33:13.

d. Isaiah in Isaiah 12:1–6.

e. Daniel in Daniel 9:3–19.

f. The psalmist in Psalm 150.

3. Perhaps the greatest prayer in the Bible is John 17. Who is praying? For what is He praying? Was His prayer effective? Has it been effective in your life?

4. What do the prayers of 1 Kings 17:21 and John 11:41–42 have in common?

5. Read Psalm 69:30–33. What pleases the Lord according to these verses? How is God glorified? What is to be our own response? What qualification is mentioned for God to hear our prayers?

More Verses to Ponder
   John 14:13–14; Romans 8:26; Acts 2:46–47; 1 Peter 2:9

A Verse to Memorize
   "And pray in the Spirit on all occasions with all kinds of prayers and requests. With this in mind, be alert and always keep on praying for all the saints." (Eph. 6:18)

My Personal Action Plan to Seek the Lord in Prayer and to Glorify Him in Thanksgiving

1.

2.

3.

4.

B

THOUGHT LIFE AND ATTITUDE

We should never underestimate the power of a thought. The mind is the wellspring of our actions and words (Prov. 4:23), and we must guard our hearts and minds from all thoughts that lead us to sin. In fact, thoughts themselves can be sinful, as Jesus has so clearly declared in the Sermon on the Mount (Matt. 5:28).

I've often considered Adam and Eve and their sin in the Garden of Eden. When did they actually commit the sin that plunged the human race into depravity and despair? Was it when they ate the fruit, or when they made the irrevocable decision to do so? Now, someone may think I'm splitting hairs, but hear me out.

Before they ate the fruit, the first couple had already decided that they loved themselves and their worldly pleasures more than they loved God. They decided that God's Word was false—that God was a liar—and they would not surely die as He had said (Gen. 2:17). They decided to commit cosmic rebellion against their Creator, the God who had lovingly placed them in such a beautiful world. Eating from the forbidden tree was almost a nonevent. Once they had decided against God, they merely took a bite of fruit.

Our attitudes also flow from our thoughts. I have been a businessman most of my life, and I can tell you that more people are promoted or fired on the basis of attitude than for any other reason. They are promoted for a good attitude, and fired for a bad one. God hates grumblers and complainers, and those who harden their hearts to His mercy and truth (Heb. 3:7–19).

A good attitude is a forgiving, loving attitude. It does not judge others harshly but sees the world through the eyes of

Christ, in mercy and compassion. God seeks to renew our minds and attitudes through His Spirit and His Word.

Matthew 5:27–29

"You have heard that it was said, 'Do not commit adultery.' But I tell you that anyone who looks at a woman lustfully has already committed adultery with her in his heart. If your right eye cause you to sin, gouge it out and throw it away. It is better to lose one part of your body than for your whole body to be thrown into hell."

Matthew 6:14–15

"For if you forgive men when they sin against you, your heavenly Father will also forgive you. But if you do not forgive men their sins, your Father will not forgive your sins."

Matthew 7:1–5

"Do not judge, or you too will be judged. For in the same way you judge others, you will be judged, and with the measure you use, it will be measured to you.

"Why do you look at the speck of sawdust in your brother's eye and pay no attention to the plank in your own eye? How can you say to your brother, 'Let me take the speck out of your eye,' when all the time there is a plank in your own eye? You hypocrite, first take the plank out of your own eye, and then you will see clearly to remove the speck from your brother's eye."

Matthew 15:10–11, 19–20

Jesus called the crowd to him and said, "Listen and understand. What goes into a man's mouth does not make him 'unclean,' but what comes out of his mouth, that is what makes him 'unclean.'" . . .

"For out of the heart come evil thoughts, murder, adultery, sexual immorality, theft, false testimony, slander.

These are what make a man 'unclean'; but eating with un-
washed hands does not make him 'unclean.'" [Cf. Mark
7:17–23.]

Matthew 22:36–37

[A Pharisee asked Jesus,] "Teacher, which is the greatest
commandment in the Law?"

Jesus replied: "'Love the Lord your God with all your
heart and with all your soul and with all your mind.'" [Cf.
Mark 12:30; Luke 10:27.]

Acts 17:30b

But now [God] commands all people everywhere to repent.

Romans 12:2

Do not conform any longer to the pattern of this world, but
be transformed by the renewing of your mind. Then you will
be able to test and approve what God's will is—his good,
pleasing and perfect will.

Romans 14:5b

[Regarding questionable matters,] each one should be fully
convinced in his own mind.

1 Corinthians 1:10

I appeal to you, brothers, in the name of our Lord Jesus
Christ, that all of you agree with one another so that there
may be no divisions among you and that you may be perfectly united in mind and thought.

1 Corinthians 4:2–5

Now it is required that those who have been given a trust
must prove faithful. I care very little whether I am judged by
you or by any human court; indeed, I do not even judge myself. My conscience is clear, but that does not make me innocent. It is the Lord who judges me. Therefore judge noth-

ing before the appointed time; wait until the Lord comes. He will bring to light what is hidden in darkness and will expose the motives of men's hearts. At that time each will receive his praise from God.

1 Corinthians 10:10
And do not grumble, as some of [the desert wanderers] did—and were killed by the destroying angel.

2 Corinthians 10:5b
. . . we take captive every thought to make it obedient to Christ.

Ephesians 4:17
So I tell you this, and insist on it in the Lord, that you must no longer live as the Gentiles do, in the futility of their thinking.

Ephesians 4:22–24
You were taught, with regard to your former way of life, to put off your old self, which is being corrupted by its deceitful desires; to be made new in the attitudes of your minds; and to put on the new self, created to be like God in true righteousness and holiness.

Ephesians 4:28a
He who has been stealing must [repent and] steal no longer.
. . .

Ephesians 4:31
Get rid of all bitterness, rage and anger, brawling and slander, along with every form of malice.

Ephesians 4:32
Be kind and compassionate to one another, forgiving each other, just as in Christ God forgave you.

Philippians 2:5 *(KJV)*
Let this mind be in you, which was also in Christ Jesus.

Philippians 4:8–9
Finally, brothers, whatever is true, whatever is noble, whatever is right, whatever is pure, whatever is lovely, whatever is admirable—if anything is excellent or praiseworthy—think about such things. Whatever you have learned or received or heard from me, or seen in me—put it into practice. And the God of peace will be with you.

Colossians 3:1–4
Since, then, you have been raised with Christ, set your hearts on things above, where Christ is seated at the right hand of God. Set your minds on things above, not on earthly things. For you died, and your life is now hidden with Christ in God. When Christ, who is your life, appears, then you also will appear with him in glory.

Hebrews 3:1
Therefore, holy brothers, who share in the heavenly calling, fix your thoughts on Jesus, the apostle and high priest whom we confess.

1 Peter 1:13–16
Therefore, prepare your minds for action; be self-controlled; set your hope fully on the grace to be given you when Jesus Christ is revealed. As obedient children, do not conform to the evil desires you had when you lived in ignorance. But just as he who called you is holy, so be holy in all you do; for it is written: "Be holy, because I am holy."

1 Peter 2:11
Dear friends, I urge you, as aliens and strangers in the world, to abstain from sinful desires, which war against your soul.

1 Peter 4:1

Therefore, since Christ suffered in his body, arm yourselves also with the same attitude, because he who has suffered in his body is done with sin.

STUDY QUESTIONS AND EXERCISES

1. Study Proverbs 7. What happens to the foolish young man? How does the woman lure him? How could he have avoided the situation?

2. According to 1 Samuel 16:7, how does the Lord judge a man? How is that different from us? What does this verse tell us about God's ability to read our very thoughts?

3. In Acts 8:9–25, we learn of Peter's rebuke of Simon the Sorcerer. What was Simon's core problem? Were his thoughts sinful? How, in verse 23, had his thoughts affected his attitude?

4. How does the Bible tell us Job dealt with his problem of lust in Job 31:1? Will the same work for you and me?

5. Daniel 1:8 gives us Daniel's method for dealing with a similar issue. What did Daniel do?

6. Philippians 4:8 speaks of our thought life. Specifically, Paul instructs us to think on true, noble, right, pure, lovely, admirable, excellent, and praiseworthy things. Make a list of things to think on that reflect those qualities. What thoughts should be avoided according to Paul's list? What will be the result of putting Paul's list into practice?

More Verses to Ponder
2 Chronicles 12:13–14; Proverbs 4:23; Romans 2:5, 14–16

A Verse to Memorize
"Do not conform any longer to the pattern of this world, but be transformed by the renewing of your mind. Then you will be able to test and approve what God's will is—his good, pleasing and perfect will." (Rom. 12:2)

My Personal Action Plan to Be Renewed in My Mind

1.

2.

3.

4.

Chapter 7

The Christian's Trust in God

The major part of biblically defined faith is trust in God. Do we really believe that God is completely in control of all events, or do we just pay lip service to His sovereignty over creation? Do we truly trust God to provide for us as His children and to carry out His purposes in and for us? We can know the answers to those questions by simply observing our lives. Do we carry in our hearts extraordinary fear? Do we worry extensively about the future? Are we powder kegs of anger only awaiting someone or something to ignite our short fuses? This chapter will look at these issues.

FEAR AND WORRY

The command "Do not be afraid" is given more times by our Lord Jesus than any other. I counted 19. There are probably more. Why should we not fear or worry about the future? Because when we fear people or life's circumstances, we attribute weakness to our all-powerful God. It is a form of idolatry.

Suppose Christ were to walk into the room where you are right now and say, "Nothing will ever happen to you that is ultimately bad." Would you ever worry again? Well, He has already said that through the apostle Paul in Romans 8:28: "And we know that in all things God works for the good of those who love him, who have been called according to his purpose." He is not saying that nothing bad will ever happen, but that what appears to be bad will ultimately work itself out for our benefit.

My favorite Bible verses are Proverbs 3:5–6: "Trust in the LORD with all your heart and lean not on your own understanding; in all your ways acknowledge him, and he will make your paths straight." It is the Old Testament version of Romans 8:28.

Another, similar, Old Testament verse is Isaiah 43:1–2.

> But now, this is what the LORD says—
> he who created you, O Jacob,
> he who formed you, O Israel:
> "Fear not, for I have redeemed you;
> I have summoned you by name; you are mine.
> When you pass through the waters,
> I will be with you;
> and when you pass through the rivers,
> they will not sweep over you.
> When you walk through the fire,
> you will not be burned;
> the flames will not set you ablaze."

God loves you and has the power to keep you safe. Trust in Him. Rest in Him. That is the highest form of worship and the source of joy.

Matthew 6:25–34

"Therefore I tell you, do not worry about your life, what you will eat or drink; or about your body, what you will wear. Is not life more important than food, and the body more important than clothes? Look at the birds of the air; they do not sow or reap or store away in barns, and yet your heavenly Father feeds them. Are you not much more valuable than they? Who of you by worrying can add a single hour to his life?

"And why do you worry about clothes? See how the lilies of the field grow. They do not labor or spin. Yet I tell you that not even Solomon in all his splendor was dressed like one of these. If that is how God clothes the grass of the field, which is here today and tomorrow is thrown into the fire, will he not much more clothe you, O you of little faith? So do not worry, saying, 'What shall we eat?' or 'What shall we drink?' or 'What shall we wear?' For the pagans run after all these things, and your heavenly Father knows that you need them. But seek first his kingdom and his righteousness, and all these things will be given to you as well. Therefore do not worry about tomorrow, for tomorrow will worry about itself. Each day has enough trouble of its own." [Cf. Luke 12:22–34]

Matthew 10:26a, 28–31

"So do not be afraid of [those who persecute you.] . . . Do not be afraid of those who kill the body but cannot kill the soul. Rather, be afraid of the One who can destroy both body and soul in hell. Are not two sparrows sold for a penny? Yet not one of them will fall to the ground apart from the will of your Father. And even the very hairs of your head are all numbered. So don't be afraid; you are worth more than many sparrows."

Mark 13:11

"Whenever you are arrested and brought to trial, do not worry beforehand about what to say. Just say whatever is given you at the time, for it is not you speaking, but the Holy Spirit." [Cf. Luke 12:11–12; Luke 21:14–15.]

John 14:1

"Do not let your hearts be troubled. Trust in God; trust also in me."

John 14:27

Peace I leave with you; my peace I give you. I do not give to you as the world gives. Do not let your hearts be troubled and do not be afraid.

Philippians 4:6–7

Do not be anxious about anything, but in everything, by prayer and petition, with thanksgiving, present your requests to God.

And the peace of God, which transcends all understanding, will guard your hearts and your minds in Christ Jesus.

1 Peter 3:13–15a

Who is going to harm you if you are eager to do good? But even if you should suffer for what is right, you are blessed. "Do not fear what they fear, do not be frightened." But in your hearts set apart Christ as Lord.

1 Peter 5:6–7

Humble yourselves, therefore, under God's mighty hand, that he may lift you up in due time. Cast all your anxiety on him because he cares for you.

STUDY QUESTIONS AND EXERCISES

1. Read John 12:42–43. Why wouldn't the Pharisees confess faith in Christ? What was their first love? Have you ever been motivated as they were?

2. Read John 19:1–13. What was Pilate's motivation for allowing Christ to be crucified? What did Jesus say of Pilate's ability to crucify Him? How does His statement refer to you?

3. Read Numbers 13:26–14:24. What was the sin of the Israelites? What was their punishment? What did God think of Joshua and Caleb?

4. Read Luke 8:22–25. Why were the disciples afraid? Were they wrong to be afraid in a situation like that? Would you be? What did Jesus do? What did He say to them? What was their reaction? What does this incident tell us about God's sovereignty over creation? About Jesus as truly God?

5. Some questions for reflection or discussion:

    a. Is it ever okay to be afraid? When?

    b. When is fear a sign of lack of faith?

    c. Is it ever okay to worry? What are we saying to God when we worry?

    d. Read Proverbs 28:1 together. Why would the wicked flee for no reason? What would give the righteous man boldness?

More Verses to Ponder

Genesis 15:1–6; Psalm 118:6; Isaiah 41:10–13; Hebrews 13:5–6

A Verse to Memorize

"Do not be afraid, little flock, for your Father has been pleased to give you the kingdom." (Luke 12:32)

My Personal Action Plan to Stop Worrying and to Trust God

1.

2.

3.

4.

B

ANGER, REVENGE, AND RESPONSE TO PERSECUTION

One afternoon not long ago, I left an R. C. Sproul seminar on the topic of anger and was driving to another Bible study about two miles away. Real spiritual of me, right? Maybe not. All of a sudden a speeder cut in front of me, almost clipping my front bumper. My right hand shot up and I began hurling expletives at the man, who by then was long gone. After I calmed down, I began to reflect on why I had blown my stack, and the irony of it all. I realized how close anger and the desire for revenge lay to the surface of my mind.

The topics of anger and revenge are very closely related to fear and worry. Why? Because God is controlling all the circumstances of this world. If everything is working to my good, when I get angry because of circumstances in my life, I am really saying to God, "I don't like the way You're running things, Lord!" My real anger is against Him.

Now, I realize that freeway driving is hazardous, and we react quickly when our lives are placed in jeopardy. But most of our anger stems from pride, and the frustration of having our little plans and dreams interrupted or thwarted. We get angry when we are slighted, or when we do not get the credit we think we deserve. Such anger is of sin, not faith.

To be sure, there is righteous anger—such as when we see God's name and Word being defamed, or when we witness injustice. But such anger is (or should be) under control and should urge us toward good works, never to consider revenge. Some of us may be called to really suffer for our faith. As Peter demonstrates in 1 Peter 4:12–19, our response to such persecution should be joy, not anger. Likewise, we are to pray for those who cut us off on the freeway. We are to bless and not curse.

Matthew 5:21–22

"You have heard that it was said to the people long ago, 'Do not murder, and anyone who murders will be subject to judgment.' But I tell you that anyone who is angry with his brother will be subject to judgment. Again, anyone who says to his brother, 'Raca,' is answerable to the Sanhedrin. But anyone who says, 'You fool!' will be in danger of the fire of hell."

Matthew 5:38–45

"You have heard that it was said, 'Eye for eye, and tooth for tooth.' But I tell you, do not resist an evil person. If someone strikes you on the right cheek, turn to him the other also. And if someone wants to sue you and take your tunic, let him have your cloak as well. If someone forces you to go one mile, go with him two miles. Give to the one who asks you, and do not turn away from the one who wants to borrow from you.

You have heard that it was said, 'Love your neighbor and hate your enemy.' But I tell you: Love your enemies and pray for those who persecute you, that you may be sons of your Father in heaven. He causes his sun to rise on the evil and the good, and sends rain on the righteous and the unrighteous."

Matthew 7:1–5

"Do not judge, or you too will be judged. For in the same way you judge others, you will be judged, and with the measure you use, it will be measured to you.

"Why do you look at the speck of sawdust in your brother's eye and pay no attention to the plank in your own eye? How can you say to your brother, 'Let me take the speck out of your eye,' when all the time there is a plank in your own eye? You hypocrite, first take the plank out of your own eye, and then you will see clearly to remove the speck from your brother's eye."

Romans 12:12b, 14

[Be] patient in affliction. . . . Bless those who persecute you; bless and do not curse.

Romans 12:17–21

Do not repay anyone evil for evil. Be careful to do what is right in the eyes of everybody. If it is possible, as far as it depends on you, live at peace with everyone. Do not take revenge, my friends, but leave room for God's wrath, for it is written: "It is mine to avenge; I will repay," says the Lord. On the contrary:

> "If your enemy is hungry, feed him;
>   if he is thirsty, give him something to drink.
> In doing this, you will heap burning coals on his
>   head."

Do not be overcome by evil, but overcome evil with good.

1 Corinthians 5:8

Therefore let us keep the Festival, not with the old yeast, the yeast of malice and wickedness, but with bread without yeast, the bread of sincerity and truth.

1 Corinthians 6:7–8

The very fact that you have lawsuits among you means you have been completely defeated already. Why not rather be wronged? Why not rather be cheated? Instead, you yourselves cheat and do wrong, and you do this to your brothers.

Ephesians 4:26–27

"In your anger do not sin": Do not let the sun go down while you are still angry, and do not give the devil a foothold.

Ephesians 4:31

Get rid of all bitterness, rage and anger, brawling and slander, along with every form of malice.

Colossians 3:8
But now you must rid yourself of all such things as these: anger, rage, malice, slander, and filthy language from your lips.

1 Thessalonians 5:15
Make sure that nobody pays back wrong for wrong, but always try to be kind to each other and to everyone else.

1 Timothy 2:8
I want men everywhere to lift up holy hands in prayer, without anger or disputing.

Hebrews 12:15
See to it that no one misses the grace of God and that no bitter root grows up to cause trouble and defile many.

James 1:19
My dear brothers, take note of this: Everyone should be quick to listen, slow to speak and slow to become angry.

1 Peter 2:21–23
To this you were called, because Christ suffered for you, leaving you an example, that you should follow in his steps.

"He committed no sin,
    and no deceit was found in his mouth."

When they hurled their insults at him, he did not retaliate; when he suffered, he made no threats. Instead, he entrusted himself to him who judges justly.

1 Peter 3:8–9a
Finally, all of you, live in harmony with one another; be sympathetic, love as brothers, be compassionate and humble. Do not repay evil with evil or insult with insult, but with blessing.

1 Peter 4:12–19

Dear friends, do not be surprised at the painful trial you are suffering, as though something strange were happening to you. But rejoice that you participate in the sufferings of Christ, so that you may be overjoyed when his glory is revealed. If you are insulted because of the name of Christ, you are blessed, for the Spirit of glory and of God rests on you. If you suffer, it should not be as a murderer or thief or any other kind of criminal, or even as a meddler. However, if you suffer as a Christian, do not be ashamed, but praise God that you bear that name. For it is time for judgment to begin with the family of God; and if it begins with us, what will the outcome be for those who do not obey the gospel of God? And,

> "If it is hard for the righteous to be saved,
>   what will become of the ungodly and the sinner?"

So then, those who suffer according to God's will should commit themselves to their faithful Creator and continue to do good.

Study Questions and Exercises

1. Read the story of Jonah. In Jonah 4:1 we read that Jonah became angry. Why? With whom was he angry? Then he became even more angry—"enough to die" (v. 9). Why? How are we sometimes like Jonah?

2. Genesis 34 tells of an act of revenge by the sons of Jacob on the Shechemites. What caused their anger? Did they act responsibly? Do you think Simeon and Levi went overboard? Have you ever sought vengeance against someone? Did you want to just get even or to get back more than you had lost? Why do you think God orders us not to take revenge?

3. In Acts 6 and 7, we are given the story of the first Christian martyr, Stephen. How did he die? What was Stephen's reaction to those who persecuted him? Have you ever suffered persecution for your faith? What was your reaction to it?

4. Read 2 Samuel 16:5–14. David is cursed by one of his subjects. What action did David take against the man? Why? Whom did David trust?

5. Read Luke 9:51–54. Why did James and John become angry and want revenge? What sin (or sins) do you suppose lay underneath their desire for revenge? (Consider John 4:9 in your answer.) Would their revenge have been just? What words do you suppose the Lord used in His rebuke of the brothers?

More Verses to Ponder
Leviticus 19:18; Proverbs 20:22; 22:24–25; 24:29; Ecclesiastes 7:9

A Verse to Memorize
"Get rid of all bitterness, rage and anger, brawling and slander, along with every form of malice." (Eph. 4:31)

My Personal Action Plan to Give My Anger to the Lord

1.

2.

3.

4.

Chapter 8

The Christian and the World

Of all the sins of the mind, pride is the most pervasive and insidious. In many ways, pride is the root sin from which all other sin flows. But our Lord was humble. Even though He created all things and is the reason they exist, He lowered Himself and came to earth as a homeless baby in order later to suffer and die in our behalf. We humans, on the other hand, have nothing that we have not received from Him (1 Cor. 4:7), and yet, without His saving grace, we lift up our noses and scoff at His holy name. It is pride that overflows in us to form greed—covetousness—and worldly ambition as we seek after fortune and fame.

PRIDE AND HUMILITY

Another of my favorite verses in Scripture is Jeremiah 9:23–24: "This is what the LORD says: 'Let not the wise man boast of his wisdom or the strong man boast of his strength or the rich man boast of his riches, but let him who boasts boast about this: that he understands and knows me, that I am the LORD, who exercises kindness, justice and righteousness on earth, for in these I delight.'"

One of humanity's common traits is the desire to boast about what one is or has. Even "the sluggard is wiser in his own eyes than seven men who answer discreetly" (Prov. 26:16). The verses in Jeremiah counter that basic, sinful inclination, and tell us instead to boast only in knowing and understanding the Lord. But there is irony here.

The person who truly knows and understands the Lord will not even boast in having arrived at that knowledge. To understand the Lord is to fall down before Him in deep humility and awe. Surely we rejoice that we know Him; as Paul says, "Let him who boasts boast in the Lord" (2 Cor. 10:17). But how did we come to know the Lord? We did not choose Him; He chose us (Deut. 10:15; John 15:16). And He chose us not because we were special in some way, but because we were lowly and despised sinners, "so that no one may boast before him" (1 Cor. 1:26–31).

Our Lord Jesus is our great example in matters of humility. He who created and sustains the universe and everything in it (Heb. 1:1–3) "made himself nothing ["of no reputation" in the KJV], taking the very nature of a servant, being made in human likeness. And being found in appearance as a man, he humbled himself and became obedient to death—even death on a cross" (Phil. 2:7–8).

Therefore, "humble yourselves before the Lord, and he will lift you up" (James 4:10).

Matthew 6:1a

"Be careful not to do your 'acts of righteousness' before men, to be seen by them."

Matthew 18:1–4

At that time the disciples came to Jesus and asked, "Who is the greatest in the kingdom of heaven?"

He called a little child and had him stand among them. And he said: "I tell you the truth, unless you change and become like little children, you will never enter the kingdom of heaven. Therefore, whoever humbles himself like this child is the greatest in the kingdom of heaven."

Matthew 20:25–28

Jesus called [the disciples] together and said, "You know that the rulers of the Gentiles lord it over them, and their high officials exercise authority over them. Not so with you. Instead, whoever wants to become great among you must be your servant, and whoever wants to be first must be your slave—just as the Son of Man did not come to be served, but to serve, and to give his life as a ransom for many." [Cf. Luke 22:24–30.]

Matthew 23:5–12

"Everything [the teachers of the law and Pharisees] do is done for men to see: . . . they love the place of honor at banquets and the most important seats in the synagogues; they love to be greeted in the marketplaces and to have men call them 'Rabbi.'

"But you are not to be called 'Rabbi,' for you have only one Master and you are all brothers. And do not call anyone on earth 'father,' for you have one Father, and he is in heaven. Nor are you to be called 'teacher,' for you have one Teacher, the Christ. The greatest among you will be your servant. For whoever exalts himself will be humbled, and whoever humbles himself will be exalted."

Luke 14:7–11

When [Jesus] noticed how the guests picked the places of honor at the table, he told them this parable: "When someone invites you to a wedding feast, do not take the place of honor, for a person more distinguished than you may have been invited. If so, the host who invited both of you will come and say to you, 'Give this man your seat.' Then, humiliated, you will have to take the least important place. But when you are invited, take the lowest place, so that when your host comes, he will say to you, 'Friend, move up to a better place.' Then you will be honored in the presence of all your fellow guests. For everyone who exalts himself will be humbled, and he who humbles himself will be exalted."

Luke 17:7–10

"Suppose one of you had a servant plowing or looking after the sheep. Would he say to the servant when he comes in from the field, 'Come along now and sit down to eat'? Would he not rather say, 'Prepare my supper, get yourself ready and wait on me while I eat and drink; after that you may eat and drink'? Would he thank the servant because he did what he was told to do? So you also, when you have done everything you were told to do, should say, 'We are unworthy servants; we have only done our duty.'"

Luke 18:9–14

To some who were confident of their own righteousness and looked down on everybody else, Jesus told this parable: "Two men went up to the temple to pray, one a Pharisee and the other a tax collector. The Pharisee stood up and prayed about himself: 'God, I thank you that I am not like all other men—robbers, evildoers, adulterers—or even like this tax collector. I fast twice a week and give a tenth of all I get.'

"But the tax collector stood at a distance. He would not even look up to heaven, but beat his breast and said, 'God, have mercy on me, a sinner.'

"I tell you that this man, rather than the other, went home justified before God. For everyone who exalts himself will be humbled, and he who humbles himself will be exalted."

John 13:13–17

[After washing his disciples' feet, Jesus said,] "You call me 'Teacher' and 'Lord,' and rightly so, for that is what I am. Now that I, your Lord and Teacher, have washed your feet, you also should wash one another's feet. I have set you an example that you should do as I have done for you. I tell you the truth, no servant is greater than his master, nor is a messenger greater than the one who sent him. Now that you know these things, you will be blessed if you do them."

Romans 12:3

For by the grace given me I say to every one of you: Do not think of yourself more highly than you ought, but rather think of yourself with sober judgment, in accordance with the measure of faith God has given you.

Romans 12:10

Be devoted to one another in brotherly love. Honor one another above yourselves.

Romans 12:16

Live in harmony with one another. Do not be proud, but be willing to associate with people of low position. Do not be conceited.

1 Corinthians 3:18–21a

Do not deceive yourselves. If any one of you thinks he is wise by the standards of this age, he should become a "fool" so that he may become wise. For the wisdom of this world is foolishness in God's sight. As it is written: "He catches the wise in their craftiness"; and again, "The Lord knows that the thoughts of the wise are futile." So then, no more boasting about men!

1 Corinthians 10:12

So, if you think you are standing firm, be careful that you don't fall!

Galatians 5:26

Let us not become conceited, provoking and envying one another.

Ephesians 4:2–3

Be completely humble and gentle; be patient, bearing with one another in love. Make every effort to keep the unity of the Spirit through the bond of peace.

Ephesians 5:21

Submit to one another out of reverence for Christ.

Philippians 2:3–8

Do nothing out of selfish ambition or vain conceit, but in humility consider others better than yourselves. Each of you should look not only to your own interests, but also to the interests of others.

Your attitude should be the same as that of Christ Jesus:

Who, being in very nature God,
   did not consider equality with God something to be
      grasped,
but made himself nothing,
   taking the very nature of a servant,
   being made in human likeness.
And being found in appearance as a man,
   he humbled himself
   and became obedient to death—
      even death on a cross.

Colossians 3:12

Therefore, as God's chosen people, holy and dearly loved, clothe yourselves with compassion, kindness, humility, gentleness and patience.

1 Timothy 6:17

Command those who are rich in this present world not to be arrogant nor to put their hope in wealth, which is so uncertain, but to put their hope in God, who richly provides us with everything for our enjoyment.

James 1:9–10

The brother in humble circumstances ought to take pride in his high position. But the one who is rich should take pride in his low position, because he will pass away like a wild flower.

James 1:21

Therefore, get rid of all moral filth and the evil that is so prevalent and humbly accept the word planted in you, which can save you.

James 3:13–17

Who is wise and understanding among you? Let him show it by his good life, by deeds done in the humility that comes from wisdom. But if you harbor bitter envy and selfish ambition in your hearts, do not boast about it or deny the truth. Such "wisdom" does not come down from heaven but is earthly, unspiritual, of the devil. For where you have envy and selfish ambition, there you will find disorder and every evil practice.

But the wisdom that comes down from heaven is first of all pure; then peace-loving, considerate, submissive, full of mercy and good fruit, impartial and sincere.

James 4:7a, 10

Submit yourselves, then, to God. . . . Humble yourselves before the Lord, and he will lift you up.

1 Peter 5:5–6

Young men, in the same way be submissive to those who are older. All of you, clothe yourselves with humility toward one another, because,

> "God opposes the proud
>   but gives grace to the humble."

Humble yourselves, therefore, under God's mighty hand, that he may lift you up in due time.

STUDY QUESTIONS AND EXERCISES

1. The Lord appeared to Solomon in a dream in 1 Kings 3:6–15. What took place? What was the attitude of Solomon's heart? How was he changed? Was God pleased?

2. Now read the account of Solomon's son Rehoboam in 1 Kings 12:1–19. How did Rehoboam's attitude differ from his father's at the beginning of his reign? What did he do? What was the result? Have you (or someone you've known) ever treated others in a similar way? What was the result?

3. In Daniel 2, Nebuchadnezzar has a troubling dream, which he demands to be reiterated and interpreted. Daniel does so, but won't boast in it. What do verses 19–30 tell us of this man Daniel? Of his relationship to the Lord?

4. In Matthew 15:21–28, Jesus has an encounter with a Canaanite woman. He seemingly insults her! What is her reaction? How does she exemplify humility? To what does Jesus liken her humility in verse 28?

5. In Romans 7:18, does Paul find within himself any good of which to boast? What about you?

More Verses to Ponder
Psalm 37:11; Proverbs 3:34; 11:2; 15:33; 25:6–7; Isaiah 66:2

A Verse to Memorize

"Humble yourselves, therefore, under God's mighty hand, that he may lift you up in due time." (1 Peter 5:6)

My Personal Action Plan to Humble Myself Before the Lord

1.

2.

3.

4.

$$\mathcal{B}$$

GREED AND WORLDLY AMBITION

How do you define success? Many people define success in terms of this world's possessions and positions. Unfortunately, many Christians have joined them in the materialistic "rat race." I, too, have been caught up in the same thing.

When I was a brand-new Christian over twenty-five years ago, I told God, "Lord, you were smart to save old Beasley! I'm going to cut a wide swath for You in the real estate development business. And, I'm going to cut Your church in on a big share of the profits!" Who was I kidding? Certainly not God. I was in it for Beasley, using God as my "ace in the hole" to assure my "success" in the world.

God then proceeded to take me not to profitability but to deep indebtedness. It took over 20 years to get my financial head above water again. But I found success! "Where?" someone asks. In the discipline of my heavenly Father.

Those who love the world system plow vainly ahead, seeking the treasures that the world has to offer. But I found out that what the world has it gives begrudgingly, if at all. And once you have its treasures, at least four things happen. First, the "treasure" is never as good as you thought. Second, you become addicted, as a little treasure causes you to seek more and more. Third, you worry about losing what treasure you've achieved. Fourth, you realize that you can't take your treasure with you when you die. I call it the "short view" of life.

God's view is the "long view." First, God's treasure is better than advertised. Second, it brings contentment. Third, God's treasure brings peace and assurance. Fourth, His treasure is eternal. You can take it with you! Seek God's treasure, and let Him define "success" for you.

Matthew 6:19–20, 24

"Do not store up for yourselves treasures on earth, where moth and rust destroy, and where thieves break in and steal. But store up for yourselves treasures in heaven, where moth and rust do not destroy, and where thieves do not break in and steal. For where your treasure is, there your heart will be also. . . . [Cf. Luke 12:33.]

"No one can serve two masters. Either he will hate the one and love the other, or he will be devoted to the one and despise the other. You cannot serve both God and Money." [Cf. Luke 16:13.]

Luke 12:15–21

Then he said to them, "Watch out! Be on your guard against all kinds of greed; a man's life does not consist in the abundance of his possessions."

And he told them this parable: "The ground of a certain rich man produced a good crop. He thought to himself, 'What shall I do? I have no place to store my crops.'

"Then he said, 'This is what I'll do. I will tear down my

barns and build bigger ones, and there I will store all my grain and my goods. And I'll say to myself, "You have plenty of good things laid up for many years. Take life easy; eat, drink, and be merry."'

"But God said to him, 'You fool! This very night your life will be demanded from you. Then who will get what you have prepared for yourself?'

"This is how it will be with anyone who stores up things for himself but is not rich toward God."

John 6:27

"Do not work for food that spoils, but for food that endures to eternal life, which the Son of Man will give you. On him God the Father has placed his seal of approval."

1 Corinthians 5:11

But now I am writing you that you must not associate with anyone who calls himself a brother but is sexually immoral or greedy, an idolater or a slanderer, a drunkard or a swindler. With such a man do not even eat.

Ephesians 5:3

But among you there must not be even a hint of sexual immorality, or of any kind of impurity, or of greed, because these are improper for God's holy people.

Colossians 3:1–5

Since, then, you have been raised with Christ, set your hearts on things above, where Christ is seated at the right hand of God. Set your minds on things above, not on earthly things. For you died, and your life is now hidden with Christ in God. When Christ, who is your life, appears, then you also will appear with him in glory.

Put to death, therefore, whatever belongs to your earthly nature: sexual immorality, impurity, lust, evil desires and greed, which is idolatry.

1 Timothy 6:3–10

If anyone teaches false doctrines and does not agree to the sound instruction of our Lord Jesus Christ and to godly teaching, he is conceited and understands nothing. He has an unhealthy interest in controversies and quarrels about words that result in envy, strife, malicious talk, evil suspicions and constant friction between men of corrupt mind, who have been robbed of the truth and who think that godliness is a means to financial gain.

But godliness with contentment is great gain. For we brought nothing into the world, and we can take nothing out of it. But if we have food and clothing, we will be content with that. People who want to get rich fall into temptation and a trap and into many foolish and harmful desires that plunge men into ruin and destruction. For the love of money is a root of all kinds of evil. Some people, eager for money, have wandered from the faith and pierced themselves with many griefs.

1 Timothy 6:17

Command those who are rich in this present world not to be arrogant nor to put their hope in wealth, which is so uncertain, but to put their hope in God, who richly provides us with everything for our enjoyment.

Titus 1:7

Since an overseer is entrusted with God's work, he must be blameless—not overbearing, not quick-tempered, not given to drunkenness, not violent, not pursuing dishonest gain.

Hebrews 13:5

Keep your lives free from the love of money and be content with what you have, because God has said,

> "Never will I leave you;
>   never will I forsake you."

James 3:13–16

Who is wise and understanding among you? Let him show it by his good life, by deeds done in the humility that comes from wisdom. But if you harbor bitter envy and selfish ambition in your hearts, do not boast about it or deny the truth. Such "wisdom" does not come down from heaven but is earthly, unspiritual, of the devil. For where you have envy and selfish ambition, there you find disorder and every evil practice.

James 4:1–4

What cause fights and quarrels among you? Don't they come from your desires that battle within you? You want something but don't get it. You kill and covet, but you cannot have what you want. You quarrel and fight. You do not have because you do not ask God. When you ask, you do not receive, because you ask with wrong motives, that you may spend what you get on your pleasures.

You adulterous people, don't you know that friendship with the world is hatred toward God? Anyone who chooses to be a friend of the world becomes an enemy of God.

1 Peter 5:2

[You elders] be shepherds of God's flock that is under your care, serving as overseers—not because you must, but because you are willing, as God wants you to be; not greedy for money, but eager to serve. . . .

1 John 2:15–17

Do not love the world or anything in the world. If anyone loves the world, the love of the Father is not in him. For everything in the world—the cravings of sinful man, the lust of his eyes and the boasting of what he has and does—comes not from the Father but from the world. The world and its desires pass away, but the man who does the will of God lives forever.

STUDY QUESTIONS AND EXERCISES

1. Human problems may be traced all the way back to the Garden of Eden. Read Genesis 3:6. What three things did Eve see in the fruit that caused her to eat of it? She was exhibiting:

   a. The _____ of the _____.

   b. The _____ of the _____.

   c. The _____ of the _____.

   (Hint: See 1 John 2:16 in the KJV.)

2. In Joshua 7, we are given the account of Achan's sin. What was it? Why do you suppose he did it? Did it bring grief to his family? Was the outcome of his action different from what he had intended? Have you (or has someone you know) ever done something like Achan did? Were the consequences different? How?

3. Read Acts 8:9–24. Why do you suppose Simon wanted the Holy Spirit? Have you ever used God as your "ace in the hole"? What happened?

4. What reason does Proverbs 23:4–5 give us for not laboring for riches?

5. Why do you think Proverbs 27:21 is true (apart from it being part of God's Word)? Why is a person "tested by the praise he receives"?

6. Read John 5:41–44. What is Jesus saying to us here about whom we should seek to please? Do you always try to please others, or is God the only one from whom you seek praise? What does Paul have to say about this issue in Galatians 1:10?

More Verses to Ponder

Job 31:24–28; Proverbs 15:27; Ecclesiastes 5:10–11; Jude 11

A Verse to Memorize

"For all that is in the world, the lust of the flesh, and the lust of the eyes, and the pride of life, is not of the Father, but is of the world." (1 John 2:16 KJV)

My Personal Action Plan to Seek the Lord's Treasure

1.

2.

3.

4.

Chapter 9

The Christian Witness

Peter wrote, "Always be prepared to give an answer to everyone who asks you to give the reason for the hope that you have" (1 Peter 3:15). Has anyone asked you to give a reason for your hope lately? Could you give a good reason if someone did? We are called to witness for Christ. But don't be intimidated by this. You don't need to be a seminary graduate to be Christ's witness. As a Christian, you have the high ground in every way—morally, spiritually, and logically. But first and foremost, you need to live out the hope within you, witnessing for Christ with your life and your lips. You also need to study "to present yourself to God as one approved, a workman who does not need to be ashamed and who correctly handles the word of truth" (2 Tim. 2:15).

PERSONAL EVANGELISM

An old axiom expresses the connection between personal evangelism and moral example: "What you are speaks so loudly I can't hear a word you say." In other words, to give out the gospel of Jesus Christ without a corresponding life of love for Christ and obedience to His commandments is an exercise in futility. In fact, it is worse than futile, for it has the opposite effect in revealing hypocrisy. People can usually spot a hypocrite a mile away.

Jesus commands that we be His witnesses (Acts 1:7–8). We are to "make disciples of all nations" (Matt. 28:19) for the purpose of bringing them into obedience to His Word. In this endeavor, He assures us that He will be right there with us in our work (Matt. 28:20).

As you go through His commandments regarding personal evangelism, prayerfully ask God to show you how best to make this joyful activity a central component of your daily walk with Christ, if you have not already done so.

There are many ways to become involved. A group from our church goes every Saturday morning to a local park to engage people there in conversations about eternal matters. Others participate in service and meetings at the downtown Rescue Mission. Still others carry on neighborhood evangelism, praying for those in their neighborhoods, befriending them for the glory of God. I was saved reading a book, and I want to use my writing to reach the lost, and to teach them to obey Christ.

Whatever method best suits your situation, personality, and calling, personal evangelism is a source of great joy and will bring a "full understanding of every good thing we have in Christ" (Philem. 6).

Matthew 5:13–16

"You are the salt of the earth. But if the salt loses its saltiness, how can it be made salty again? It is no longer good for anything, except to be thrown out and trampled by men.

"You are the light of the world. A city on a hill cannot be hidden. Neither do people light a lamp and put it under a bowl. Instead they put it on its stand, and it gives light to everyone in the house. In the same way, let your light shine before men, that they may see your good deeds and praise your Father in heaven."

Matthew 7:6

"Do not give dogs what is sacred; do not throw your pearls

to pigs. If you do, they may trample them under their feet, and then turn and tear you to pieces."

Matthew 28:18–20

Then Jesus came to them and said, "All authority in heaven and on earth has been given to me. Therefore go and make disciples of all nations, baptizing them in the name of the Father and of the Son and of the Holy Spirit, and teaching them to obey everything I have commanded you. And surely I am with you always, to the very end of the age." [Cf. Mark 16:15.]

Acts 1:7–8

[Jesus] said to them: "It is not for you to know the times or dates the Father has set by his own authority. But you . . . will be my witnesses in Jerusalem, and in all Judea and Samaria, and to the ends of the earth."

1 Corinthians 10:31–11:1

So whether you eat or drink or whatever you do, do it all for the glory of God. Do not cause anyone to stumble, whether Jews, Greeks or the church of God—even as I try to please everybody in every way. For I am not seeking my own good but the good of many, so that they may be saved. Follow my example, as I follow the example of Christ.

Ephesians 5:15–20

Be very careful, then, how you live—not as unwise but as wise, making the most of every opportunity, because the days are evil. Therefore do not be foolish, but understand what the Lord's will is. Do not get drunk on wine, which leads to debauchery. Instead, be filled with the Spirit. Speak to one another with psalms, hymns and spiritual songs. Sing and make music in your heart to the Lord, always giving thanks to God the Father for everything, in the name of our Lord Jesus Christ.

Colossians 4:5–6

Be wise in the way you act toward outsiders; make the most of every opportunity. Let your conversation be always full of grace, seasoned with salt, so that you may know how to answer everyone.

2 Timothy 1:8

So do not be ashamed to testify about our Lord, or ashamed of me his prisoner. But join with me in suffering for the gospel, by the power of God. . . .

Titus 2:7–8

In everything set [the young men] an example by doing what is good. In your teaching show integrity, seriousness and soundness of speech that cannot be condemned, so that those who oppose you may be ashamed because they have nothing bad to say about us.

Philemon 6

I pray that you may be active in sharing your faith, so that you will have a full understanding of every good thing we have in Christ.

Hebrews 13:13

Let us, then, go to [Jesus] outside the camp, bearing the disgrace he bore.

1 Peter 3:15–16

But in your hearts set apart Christ as Lord. Always be prepared to give an answer to everyone who asks you to give the reason for the hope that you have. But do this with gentleness and respect, keeping a clear conscience, so that those who speak maliciously against your good behavior in Christ may be ashamed of their slander.

Jude 22–23

Be merciful to those who doubt; snatch others from the fire

and save them; to others show mercy, mixed with fear—hating even the clothing stained by corrupted flesh.

STUDY QUESTIONS AND EXERCISES

1. In Matthew 23:15, Jesus speaks of the active evangelical zeal of the Pharisees and teachers of the law. But He also criticizes them sharply for other practices. What are they, both in this verse and in the rest of the chapter? What can we learn from their practices that will make our own more pleasing to God?

2. Read 1 Corinthians 2:1–5. What was the state of Paul's mind when he first witnessed to the Corinthians? Did he rely upon his own knowledge and talent? If not, on what did he rely? For what specific reason? How might these verses apply to you and me?

3. Acts 5:17–42 gives the account of Peter and the other apostles being brought before the Sanhedrin, or Jewish ruling council. What testimony did they give? What was the Sanhedrin's reaction? In verses 41 and 42, what was the result of this persecution in the apostles' hearts? In the apostles' future activity?

4. Our Lord gives a strange command in Matthew 7:6. How does this command intersect with His call to be our witnesses?

More Verses to Ponder
   John 4:1–26; Acts 8:26–40; 10:39–43; Mark 16:20

A *Verse to Memorize*

"I pray that you may be active in sharing your faith, so that you will have a full understanding of every good thing we have in Christ." (Philem. 6)

My Personal Action Plan to Be a Witness for Christ

1.

2.

3.

4.

DOCTRINE AND BIBLE STUDY

There is a growing view in Christian circles that doctrine is unimportant, that biblical understanding is secondary to one's experience. We may hear this kind of comment: "I don't need any doctrine. I just need Jesus!" But who is Jesus? The minute you ask that question, you are into doctrine.

Jesus said in Matthew 24:4–5, "Watch out that no one deceives you. For many will come in my name, claiming, 'I am the Christ,' and will deceive many." How can we be sure we are not being deceived? First, we must trust in the Bible as our only source for faith and life, sufficient for all our understanding. By it we make our "calling and election sure" (2 Peter 1:10)— we gain assurance of our salvation.

Next, we must become capable of "correctly handl[ing] the Word of truth" (2 Tim. 2:15). We just can't put the Bible on top of our heads and think that its truth will somehow trickle down by osmosis. It is hard work. We need to know proper methods of interpretation, and then apply them to our diligent study.

The Bible is a supernatural book. Its transforming truth comes only through the Holy Spirit as He opens it and applies it to our hearts and lives. Therefore, we need to approach the book prayerfully and with faith. Finally, we need to study with hearts and minds that are willing to do what the Bible commands us. If we study only for our own selfish interests or to prove our own preconceived notions, we will fail.

Our study of God's doctrine is for the purpose of being conformed to His will—to grow in the nurture and instruction of the Lord (Eph. 6:4). God's purpose for each one of His children is that they reflect His glory by becoming more like His Son day by day. Such purposes are to be fulfilled by the study of His powerful Word.

Matthew 5:17–20

"Do not think that I have come to abolish the Law or the Prophets [i.e., the Old Testament]; I have not come to abolish them but to fulfill them. I tell you the truth, until heaven and earth disappear, not the smallest letter, not the least stroke of a pen, will by any means disappear from the Law until everything is accomplished. Anyone who breaks one of the least of these commandments and teaches others to do the same will be called least in the kingdom of heaven, but whoever practices and teaches these commands will be called great in the kingdom of heaven."

Matthew 7:15–23

"Watch out for false prophets. They come to you in sheep's clothing, but inwardly they are ferocious wolves. By their fruit you will recognize them. Do people pick grapes from thorn bushes, or figs from thistles? Likewise every good tree bears good fruit, but a bad tree bears bad fruit. A good tree cannot bear bad fruit, and a bad tree cannot bear good fruit. Every tree that does not bear good fruit is cut down and thrown into the fire. Thus, by their fruit you will recognize them.

"Not everyone who says to me, 'Lord, Lord,' will enter the kingdom of heaven, but only he who does the will of my Father who is in heaven. Many will say to me on that day, 'Lord, Lord, did we not prophesy in your name, and in your name drive out demons and perform many miracles?' Then I will tell them plainly, 'I never knew you. Away from me, you evildoers!'"

Luke 21:8

[Jesus] replied, "Watch out that you are not deceived. For many will come in my name, claiming, 'I am he,' and 'The time is near.' Do not follow them."

John 4:24

"God is Spirit, and his worshippers must worship in spirit and in truth."

Romans 16:17–18

I urge you, brothers, to watch out for those who cause divisions and put obstacles in your way that are contrary to the teaching you have learned. Keep away from them. For such people are not serving our Lord Christ, but their own appetites. By smooth talk and flattery they deceive the minds of naive people.

1 Corinthians 3:10–11, 21a

By the grace God has given me, I laid a foundation as an expert builder, and someone else is building on it. But each one should be careful how he builds. For no one can lay any foundation other than the one already laid, which is Jesus Christ. . . . So then, no more boasting about men!

Galatians 1:8–9

But even if we or an angel from heaven should preach a gospel other than the one we preached to you, let him be eternally condemned! As we have already said, so now I say again: If anybody is preaching to you a gospel other than what you accepted, let him be eternally condemned!

Ephesians 6:10–11, 17

Finally, be strong in the Lord and in his mighty power. Put on the full armor of God so that you can take your stand against the devil's schemes. . . . Take the helmet of salvation and the sword of the Spirit, which is the word of God.

Colossians 2:6–8

So then, just as you received Christ Jesus as Lord, continue to live in him, rooted and built up in him, strengthened in the faith as you were taught, and overflowing with thankfulness.

See to it that no one takes you captive through hollow and deceptive philosophy, which depends on human tradition and the basic principles of this world rather than Christ.

Colossians 3:16a

Let the word of Christ dwell in you richly as you teach and admonish one another with all wisdom. . . .

1 Thessalonians 5:20

Do not treat prophecies with contempt.

1 Timothy 4:6–7

If you point these [heresies] out to the brothers, you will be a good minister of Christ Jesus, brought up in the truths of the faith and of the good teaching that you have followed. Have nothing to do with godless myths and old wives' tales; rather, train yourself to be godly.

1 Timothy 4:16

Watch your life and doctrine closely. Persevere in them, because if you do, you will save both yourself and your hearers.

1 Timothy 6:3–4a

If anyone teaches false doctrines and does not agree to the sound instruction of our Lord Jesus Christ and to godly teaching, he is conceited and understands nothing.

1 Timothy 6:20b–21

Turn away from godless chatter and the opposing ideas of what is falsely called knowledge, which some have professed and in so doing have wandered from the faith.

2 Timothy 2:14–15

Keep reminding them of these things. Warn them before God against quarreling about words; it is of no value, and only ruins those who listen. Do your best to present yourself to God as one approved, a workman who does not need to be ashamed and who correctly handles the word of truth.

Titus 2:1–2

You must teach what is in accord with sound doctrine. Teach the older men to be temperate, worthy of respect, self-controlled, and sound in faith, in love and in endurance.

Titus 3:9–11

But avoid foolish controversies and genealogies and arguments and quarrels about the law, because these are unprofitable and useless. Warn a divisive person once, and then warn him a second time. After that, have nothing to do with him. You may be sure that such a man is warped and sinful; he is self-condemned.

Hebrews 5:11–14

We have much to say about this [difficult doctrine], but it is hard to explain because you are slow to learn. In fact, though by this time you ought to be teachers, you need someone to teach you the elementary truths of God's word all over again. You need milk, not solid food! Anyone who lives on milk, being still an infant, is not acquainted with the teaching about righteousness. But solid food is for the mature, who by constant use have trained themselves to distinguish good from evil.

Hebrews 13:9a

Do not be carried away by all kinds of strange teachings.

James 1:21–25

Therefore, get rid of all moral filth and the evil that is so prevalent and humbly accept the word planted in you, which can save you.

Do not merely listen to the word, and so deceive yourselves. Do what it says. Anyone who listens to the word but does not do what it says is like a man who looks at his face in a mirror and, after looking at himself, goes away and immediately forgets what he looks like. But the man who looks intently into the perfect law that gives freedom, and continues to do this, not forgetting what he has heard, but doing it— he will be blessed in what he does.

1 Peter 2:2–3

Like newborn babies, crave pure spiritual milk, so that by it you may grow up in your salvation, now that you have tasted that the Lord is good.

1 Peter 3:15

But in your hearts set apart Christ as Lord. Always be prepared to give an answer to everyone who asks you to give the reason for the hope that you have. But do this with gentleness and respect. . . .

STUDY QUESTIONS AND EXERCISES

1. Read Psalm 119. As you come to the following verses, note what benefit is described for the serious student of the Bible.

    a. Verse 9:

    b. Verse 11:

    c. Verse 24:

    d. Verse 28:

    e. Verse 41:

    f. Verse 49:

    g. Verse 72:

    h. Verse 99:

    i. Verse 104:

    j. Verse 162:

    k. Verse 165:

2. Read Isaiah 55:10–11. God has a purpose for His Word. Do you think it is to decorate a bookshelf? How are we to know God's revealed will if we do not study His Word?

3. Read Hebrews 4:2 and 12. What is the key element to understanding the Bible found in verse 2? In verse 12, what is one of the purposes of God's Word? Will God's Word help us to understand ourselves better? To change?

4. Read Acts 17:10–12. What did the Bereans do with the Scripture? Why? How often? If you were suddenly confronted with an angel from heaven—powerful, beautiful, and full of light—and this angel told you something that you were to accept as truth, what would you do? Would you accept it without question? Would you do something else?

5. Read Luke 24:13–27. What does Jesus have to say about the Old Testament in these verses? Can you find Christ in the places He mentions? Elsewhere in the Old Testament? Look up some verses that point to Christ in the Old Testament, and bring them to class to share with others.

More Verses to Ponder
   Psalm 12:6; Proverbs 30:5; Isaiah 40:8; John 8:31–32

A Verse to Memorize
   "Do your best to present yourself to God as one approved, a workman who does not need to be ashamed and who correctly handles the word of truth." (2 Tim. 2:15)

My Personal Action Plan to Master the Word of God

1.

2.

3.

4.

Chapter 10

The Christian's Earthly Obligations

It has been said (erroneously) that the only two things certain in life are death and taxes. I would submit that there is also work. Even death is not certain for the Christian if our Lord would come soon. But taxes and work remain for the vast majority of us.

God Himself is a worker (John 5:17) and is working even today to bring about His purposes in creation. He also ordained our work, as well as the governing authorities under whom we work and live. Our earthly obligations to obey those in authority over us and to work to support ourselves and others are very important obligations to God.

OBEDIENCE TO EARTHLY AUTHORITY

God has established human government in order to provide an environment in which His purposes may be achieved on the earth. Governments exists in the political, business, church, and family spheres, as well as in organizations with which we voluntarily associate ourselves, such as schools.

The Word of God alone is able to bind our consciences—to ultimately govern all of our thoughts, words, and actions. But as long as the governing authorities do not require that we go against the proper teaching of Scripture, then we are obligated to obey the laws that are duly instituted. That includes paying taxes and helping to defend the nation of which we are citizens from foreign attack.

If, however, earthly authority requires that we act in opposition to Holy Scripture, then it is our duty not only to oppose the law but to disobey it. The abortion debate has brought this problem into focus in our own day. Our federal government allows abortions, and Christians rightly oppose the practice. But we are not being required to abort our children, as people are, for instance, in mainland China. We may oppose abortion in the United States, but we must be careful not to break the duly instituted laws of the state in our opposition to it. God requires that we work within the legal system.

The same principle is true in whatever organizational structure we find ourselves. In the church, there is to be obedience to the authorities that God has ordained (Heb. 13:17). But such obedience is not required if the demands of the organization exceed or oppose the law of God, such as manmade laws imposed upon the Jews of Jesus' day by the Pharisees and scribes.

Matthew 22:21b

[In response to the Pharisee's question, "Is it right to pay taxes to Caesar or not?" Jesus] said to them, "Give to Caesar what is Caesar's, and to God what is God's."

Romans 13:1–5

Everyone must submit himself to the governing authorities, for there is no authority except that which God has established. The authorities that exist have been established by God. Consequently, he who rebels against the authority is rebelling against what God has instituted, and those who do so will bring judgment on themselves. For rulers hold no terror for those who do right, but for those who do wrong. Do you want to be free from fear of the one in authority? Then do what is right and he will commend you. For he is God's servant to do you good. But if you do wrong, be afraid, for he does not bear the sword for nothing. He is God's servant, an agent of wrath to bring punishment on the wrongdoer. Therefore, it is necessary to submit to the authorities, not only because of possible punishment but also because of conscience.

Ephesians 5:21
Submit to one another out of reverence for Christ.

Ephesians 5:22–24
Wives, submit to your husbands as to the Lord. For the husband is the head of the wife as Christ is head of the church, his body, of which he is the Savior. Now as the church submits to Christ, so also wives should submit to their husbands in everything.

Ephesians 6:1–3
Children, obey your parents in the Lord, for this is right. "Honor your father and mother"—which is the first commandment with a promise—"that it may go well with you and that you may enjoy long life on the earth."

Ephesians 6:5–8
Slaves, obey your earthly masters with respect and fear, and with sincerity of heart, just as you would obey Christ. Obey them not only to win their favor when their eye is on you, but like slaves of Christ, doing the will of God from your heart. Serve wholeheartedly, as if you were serving the Lord, not men, because you know that the Lord will reward everyone for whatever good he does, whether he is slave or free.

1 Thessalonians 5:12–13a
Now we ask you, brothers, to respect those who work hard among you, who are over you in the Lord and who admonish you. Hold them in the highest regard in love because of their work.

1 Timothy 2:1–3

I urge, then, first of all, that requests, prayers, intercession and thanksgiving be made for everyone—for kings and all those in authority, that we may live peaceful and quiet lives in all godliness and holiness. This is good, and pleases God our Savior.

1 Timothy 5:17–20

The elders who direct the affairs of the church well are worthy of double honor, especially those whose work is preaching and teaching. For the Scripture says, "Do not muzzle the ox while it is treading out the grain," and "The worker deserves his wages." Do not entertain an accusation against an elder unless it is brought by two or three witnesses. Those who sin are to be rebuked publicly, so that the others may take warning.

Titus 3:1–2

Remind the people to be subject to rulers and authorities, to be obedient, to be ready to do whatever is good, to slander no one, to be peaceable and considerate, and to show true humility toward all men.

Hebrews 13:7–8

Remember your leaders, who spoke the word of God to you. Consider the outcome of their way of life and imitate their faith. Jesus Christ is the same yesterday and today and forever.

Hebrews 13:17

Obey your leaders and submit to their authority. They keep watch over you as men who must give an account. Obey them so that their work will be a joy, not a burden, for that would be of no advantage to you.

1 Peter 2:13–17

Submit yourselves for the Lord's sake to every authority instituted among men: whether to the king, as the supreme authority, or to governors, who are sent by him to punish those who do wrong and to commend those who do right. For it is God's will that by doing good you should silence the ignorant talk of foolish men. Live as free men, but do not use your freedom as a cover-up for evil; live as servants of God. Show proper respect to everyone: Love the brotherhood of believers, fear God, honor the king.

1 Peter 2:18–20a

Slaves, submit yourselves to your masters with all respect, not only to those who are good and considerate, but also to those who are harsh. For it is commendable if a man bears up under the pain of unjust suffering because he is conscious of God. But how is it to your credit if you receive a beating for doing wrong and endure it?

1 Peter 3:1–2

Wives, in the same way [as Christ entrusted Himself to Him who judges justly] be submissive to your husbands so that, if any of them do not believe the word, they may be won over without words by the behavior of their wives, when they see the purity and reverence of your lives.

STUDY QUESTIONS AND EXERCISES

1. In 2 Samuel 20 we are given the account of Sheba, a man who rose up in anarchy against David. Who stayed with David? Who went to Sheba's side? What happened to Sheba?

2. Two towns of Israel disregarded patriotism in Judges 8. What were their names? Whom did they oppose? What were the consequences?

3. Read Judges 21:25. What do you think America would be like if this were the case today? If you are in a study group, discuss the evils of anarchy and what we can do as citizens to make our government better.

4. What reasons does Paul give in 1 Timothy 2:1–4 as to why we should pray for and give thanks to God for our governing authorities? Why is that important for America and for the church of Jesus Christ?

5. The Romans were cruel overseers of Israel at the time of Christ. But what consequences of their administration paved the way for the rapid spread of the gospel message throughout the world?

More Verses to Ponder

Ezra 6:10; Proverbs 24:21; Ecclesiastes 8:2–4; Jeremiah 29:7

A Verse to Memorize

"Everyone must submit himself to the governing authorities, for there is no authority except that which God has established." (Rom. 13:1)

My Personal Action Plan to Obey Those in Authority over Me

1.

2.

3.

4.

$\mathcal{B}$

WORK AND BUSINESS

Some people think that work is a curse God put upon the human race because of the Fall. But a careful reading of the first chapters of Genesis reveals that it is not. God gave Adam good, meaningful work to do. He was to be ruler (1:26), a gardener (2:15), and the first scientist (2:19–20). Adam classified and gave names to all of the creatures of God.

The sin of Adam brought pain and frustration to his labor. We are told in Genesis 3:17–19 that God said to Adam, "Because you listened to your wife and ate from the tree about which I commanded you, 'You must not eat of it,' Cursed is the ground because of you; through painful toil you will eat of it all the days of your life. It will produce thorns and thistles for you, and you will eat the plants of the field. By the sweat of your brow you will eat your food. . . ."

As we learned earlier, God commands us to work six days and rest on the seventh (Ex. 20:9). Labor is not an option. Those who belong to God should be employed in His service whether on the job, in the home, or in the church. In the Middle Ages, work was classified into two separate categories: sacred and secular. Sacred work was done by the clergy. All other work was profane. The Bible does not teach such a dichotomy. All labor is sacred.

If you are like me (and everyone else), you have been frustrated in your work. Plans somehow just don't work out the way we intend. Before you throw up your hands in despair, remember that your "Job 1" is glorifying the God "who works out everything in conformity with the purpose of his will" (Eph. 1:11). "Whatever you do, work at it with all your heart, as working for the Lord, not for men, since you know you will receive an inheritance from the Lord as a reward" (Col. 3:23–24).

Acts 20:35

In everything I [Paul] did, I showed you that by this kind of hard work we must help the weak, remembering the words the Lord Jesus himself said: "It is more blessed to give than to receive."

Romans 13:8a

Let no debt remain outstanding, except the continuing debt to love one another. . . .

Ephesians 4:28

He who has been stealing must steal no longer, but must work, doing something useful with his own hands, that he may have something to share with those in need.

Ephesians 6:5–8

Slaves, obey your earthly masters with respect and fear, and with sincerity of heart, just as you would obey Christ. Obey them not only to win their favor when their eye is on you, but like slaves of Christ, doing the will of God from your heart. Serve wholeheartedly, as if you were serving the Lord, not men, because you know that the Lord will reward everyone for whatever good he does, whether he is slave or free.

Ephesians 6:9

And masters, treat your slaves in the same way. Do not threaten them, since you know that he who is both their Master and yours is in heaven, and there is no favoritism with him.

Colossians 3:22–25

Slaves, obey your earthly masters in everything; and do it, not only when their eye is on you and to win their favor, but with sincerity of heart and reverence for the Lord. Whatever you do, work at it with all your heart, as working for the Lord, not for men, since you know that you will receive an inheritance from the Lord as a reward. It is the Lord Christ you are serving. Anyone who does wrong will be repaid for his wrong, and there is no favoritism.

Colossians 4:1

Masters, provide your slaves with what is right and fair, because you know that you also have a Master in heaven.

1 Thessalonians 4:11–12

Make it your ambition to lead a quiet life, to mind your own business and to work with your hands, just as we told you, so that your daily life may win the respect of outsiders and so that you will not be dependent on anybody.

2 Thessalonians 3:6–13

In the name of the Lord Jesus Christ, we command you, brothers, to keep away from every brother who is idle and does not live according to the teaching you received from us. For you yourselves know how you ought to follow our example. We were not idle when we were with you, nor did we eat anyone's food without paying for it. On the contrary, we worked night and day, laboring and toiling so that we would not be a burden to any of you. We did this, not because we do not have the right to such help, but in order to make ourselves a model for you to follow. For even when we were with you, we gave you this rule: "If a man will not work, he shall not eat."

We hear that some among you are idle. They are not busy; they are busybodies. Such people we command and urge in the Lord Jesus Christ to settle down and earn the bread they eat. And as for you, brothers, never tire of doing what is right.

1 Timothy 5:8

If anyone does not provide for his relatives, and especially for his immediate family, he has denied the faith and is worse than an unbeliever.

1 Timothy 5:18

For the Scripture says, "Do not muzzle the ox while it is treading out the grain," and "The worker deserves his wages."

1 Timothy 6:1–2

All who are under the yoke of slavery should consider their masters worthy of full respect, so that God's name and our teaching may not be slandered. Those who have believing masters are not to show less respect for them because they are brothers. Instead, they are to serve them even better, because those who benefit from their service are believers, and dear to them. These are the things you are to teach and urge on them.

Titus 2:9–10

Teach slaves to be subject to their masters in everything, to try to please them, not to talk back to them, and not to steal from them, but to show that they can be fully trusted, so that in every way they will make the teaching about God our Savior attractive.

Titus 3:14

Our people must learn to devote themselves to doing what is good, in order that they may provide for daily necessities and not live unproductive lives.

1 Peter 2:18–20a

Slaves, submit yourselves to your masters with all respect, not only to those who are good and considerate, but also to those who are harsh. For it is commendable if a man bears up under the pain of unjust suffering because he is conscious of God. But how is it to your credit if you receive a beating for doing wrong and endure it?

STUDY QUESTIONS AND EXERCISES

1. Elisha had a servant named Gehazi. In 2 Kings 5 we are told of his activities in connection with an army officer named Naaman. What happened? What were the results for Gehazi? What principle can you draw from this episode to apply to your own life?

2. Read Matthew 20:1–16. What principle can we draw about contractual relationships from this parable of Jesus'?

3. In Ruth 2, we see Ruth going into the fields of Boaz. Boaz is a fine businessman and employer. Find and list some of Boaz' character traits as described in the book of Ruth. Compare your list to that of others.

4. What principles of business may we learn from these proverbs?

   a. 10:9

   b. 15:19

   c. 28:19

   d. 18:17

   e. 28:23

   f. 22:3

   g. 22:7

   h. 17:27–28

    i. 15:22

    j. 16:18–19

    k. 13:11

    l. 15:27

More Verses to Ponder
Proverbs 21:5; 22:9; 24:30–34; 31:27; Ecclesiastes 11:4, 6

A Verse to Memorize
"Whatever you do, work at it with all your heart, as working for the Lord, not for men, since you know that you will receive an inheritance from the Lord as a reward." (Col. 3:23–24a)

My Personal Action Plan to Be More Diligent in My Work

1.

2.

3.

4.

Chapter 11

The Christian Family

It may seem strange to some that I teamed up the topics "Godly Speech" and "Marriage and Family" in this chapter. But when you think about it, where of all places is godly speech often most difficult? Where does the tongue get most of its exercise? And, where of all places is godly speech most crucial? In the home, of course. If we can control our tongues among family members, we can control it almost anywhere. But in the final analysis, only God's Spirit can control the tongue and tame it. And only He can bring ultimate peace and joy to the family.

Godly Speech

James says,

> If anyone is never at fault in what he says, he is a perfect man, able to keep his whole body in check.
> When we put bits in the mouths of horses to make them obey us, we can turn the whole animal. Or take ships as an example. Although they are so large and are driven by strong winds, they are steered by a very small rudder wherever the pilot

wants to go. Likewise the tongue is a small part of the body, but it makes great boasts. Consider what a great forest is set on fire by a small spark. The tongue is also a fire, a world of evil among the parts of the body. It corrupts the whole person, sets the whole course of his life on fire, and is itself set on fire by hell.

All kinds of animals, birds, reptiles and creatures of the sea are being tamed and have been tamed by man, but no man can tame the tongue. It is a restless evil, full of deadly poison.

With the tongue we praise our Lord and Father, and with it we curse men, who have been made in God's likeness. Out of the same mouth come praise and cursing. My brothers, this should not be. Can both fresh water and salt water flow from the same spring? My brothers, can a fig tree bear olives, or a grapevine bear figs? Neither can a salt spring produce fresh water. (James 3:2–12)

Those verses have always made me shiver, particularly knowing that I shall give account one day for every careless word that I have uttered (Matt. 12:36–37). The old saw "Sticks and stones may break my bones, but words will never harm me" is horribly wrong. Lives are shattered by the power of words. A broken bone can be mended, but a broken spirit? We need to remember that our words are merely the outward expression of an evil heart, a heart that only Christ can cure.

Matthew 5:22

"But I tell you that anyone who is angry with his brother will be subject to judgment. Again, anyone who says to his brother, 'Raca,' is answerable to the Sanhedrin. But anyone who says, 'You fool,' will be in danger of the fire of hell."

Matthew 12:36–37

"But I tell you that men will have to give account on the day of judgment for every careless word they have spoken. For by your words you will be acquitted, and by your words you will be condemned."

Ephesians 4:25

Therefore each of you must put off falsehood and speak truthfully to his neighbor, for we are all members of one body.

Ephesians 4:29

Do not let any unwholesome talk come out of your mouths, but only what is helpful for building others up according to their needs, that it may benefit those who listen.

Ephesians 5:4

Nor should there be obscenity, foolish talk or coarse joking, which are out of place, but rather thanksgiving.

Colossians 3:8–9

But now you must rid yourselves of all such things as these: anger, rage, malice, slander, and filthy language from your lips. Do not lie to each other, since you have taken off your old self with its practices.

Colossians 4:6

Let your conversation be always full of grace, seasoned with salt, so that you may know how to answer everyone.

1 Timothy 4:11–12

Command and teach these things. Don't let anyone look down on you because you are young, but set an example for the believers in speech, in life, in love, in faith and in purity.

1 Timothy 6:20

Timothy, guard what has been entrusted to your care. Turn away from godless chatter and the opposing ideas of what is falsely called knowledge.

2 Timothy 2:14

Keep reminding them of these things. Warn them before God against quarreling about words; it is of no value, and only ruins those who listen.

2 Timothy 2:16

Avoid godless chatter, because those who indulge in it will become more and more ungodly.

Titus 3:2

. . . slander no one, [but] be peaceable and considerate, and . . . show true humility toward all men.

Hebrews 3:13

. . . encourage one another daily, as long as it is called Today, so that none of you may be hardened by sin's deceitfulness.

Hebrews 10:24–25

And let us consider how we may spur one another on toward love and good deeds. Let us not give up meeting together, as some are in the habit of doing, but let us encourage one another—and all the more as you see the Day approaching.

James 1:19

My dear brothers, take note of this: Everyone should be quick to listen, slow to speak and slow to become angry. . . .

James 1:26

If anyone considers himself religious and yet does not keep a tight rein on his tongue, he deceives himself and his religion is worthless.

James 3:9–12

With the tongue we praise our Lord and Father, and with it we curse men, who have been made in God's likeness. Out of the same mouth come praise and cursing. My brothers, this should not be. Can both fresh water and salt water flow from the same spring? My brothers, can a fig tree bear olives, or a grapevine bear figs? Neither can a salt spring produce fresh water.

James 4:11

Brothers, do not slander one another. Anyone who speaks against his brother or judges him, speaks against the law and judges it. When you judge the law, you are not keeping it, but sitting in judgment on it.

James 5:9a

Don't grumble against each other, brothers, or you will be judged.

James 5:12

Above all, my brothers, do not swear—not by heaven or by earth or by anything else. Let your "Yes" be yes, and your "No," no, or you will be condemned.

1 Peter 2:1

Therefore, rid yourselves of all malice and all deceit, hypocrisy, envy, and slander of every kind.

1 Peter 3:9–10

Do not repay evil with evil or insult with insult, but with blessing, because to this you were called so that you may inherit a blessing. For,

"Whoever would love life
  and see good days
must keep his tongue from evil
  and his lips from deceitful speech."

Study Questions and Exercises

1. Read Proverbs 6:16–19. Solomon gives us seven things that the Lord hates. How many relate to the tongue? In what way is sin manifested in each?

2. Psalm 15:1 asks the question "LORD, who may dwell in your sanctuary? Who may live on your holy hill?" What is the answer in verses 2 and 3? List those who may. How many of these descriptions deal with speech?

3. What principles may we draw from these proverbs that will guide us to a more godly way of speaking? If you are in a study group, bring your list to class for discussion.

   a. 12:19

   b. 16:21

   c. 27:2

   d. 15:23

   e. 28:23

   f. 15:1

g. 17:9

h. 12:18

i. 20:15

j. 10:19

k. 16:23

More Verses to Ponder
Psalm 141:3; Proverbs 26:20–28; Luke 6:45; Romans 1:29–30

A Verse to Memorize
"Let your conversation be always full of grace, seasoned with salt, so that you may know how to answer everyone." (Col. 4:6)

My Personal Action Plan Toward More Godly Speech

1.

2.

3.

4.

B

MARRIAGE AND FAMILY

The family was the first social organization created by God. It is fundamental to society, the place where children—future leaders—are raised and nurtured. Marriage and the family have come under attack today as in no other time in history. I don't need to fill in the details.

God is very serious about the integrity of the marriage relationship between a man and a woman, and of the family unit created by their union. The following verses deal specifically with marriage and family, but all of the commandments of Christ have application to the well-being of these relationships.

The closest relationships we will ever develop on this earth are between husbands and wives, and parents and children. Who you really are quickly becomes known under the magnifying glass of such kinship. Little sins and blunders tend to be intensified. Forgiveness is imperative, as is faithfulness, obedience, submission, servanthood—indeed, all of the characteristics that make up the love that is taught us in Scripture.

That marriage is the most crucial earthly relationship is further exemplified by its setting forth the relationship between Christ and His church (Eph. 5:32). The relationship of a husband to his wife is to reflect Christ's headship of and love for His church. Conversely, the wife is to respect her husband and be submissive to him, just as the church does the same to Jesus. While marriage partners are equals before God, He has assigned them distinct roles for their mutual good.

Matthew 5:31–32

"It has been said, 'Anyone who divorces his wife must give her a certificate of divorce.' But I tell you that anyone who divorces his wife, except for marital unfaithfulness, causes her to become an adulteress, and anyone who marries the divorced woman commits adultery."

Matthew 19:3–6

Some Pharisees came to [Jesus] to test him. They asked, "Is it lawful for a man to divorce his wife for any and every reason?"

"Haven't you read," he replied, "that at the beginning the Creator 'made them male and female,' and said, 'For this reason a man will leave his father and mother and be united to his wife, and the two will become one flesh'? So they are no longer two, but one. Therefore what God has joined together, let man not separate." [Cf. Mark 10:2–12; Luke 16:18.]

1 Corinthians 7:1–7, 10–15

Now for the matters you wrote about: It is good for a man not to marry. But since there is so much immorality, each man should have his own wife, and each woman her own husband. The husband should fulfill his marital duty to his wife, and likewise the wife to her husband. The wife's body does not belong to her alone but also to her husband. In the same way, the husband's body does not belong to him alone but also to his wife. Do not deprive each other except by mutual consent and for a time, so that you may devote yourselves to prayer. Then come together again so that Satan will not tempt you because of your lack of self-control. I say this as a concession, not as a command. I wish that all men were as I am. But each man has his own gift from God; one has this gift, another has that. . . .

To the married I give this command (not I, but the Lord): A wife must not separate from her husband. But if she does, she must remain unmarried or else be reconciled to her husband. And a husband must not divorce his wife.

To the rest I say this (I, not the Lord): If any brother has a wife who is not a believer and she is willing to live with him, he must not divorce her. And if a woman has a husband who is not a believer and he is willing to live with her, she must not divorce him. For the unbelieving husband has been sanctified through his wife, and the unbelieving wife has been sanctified through her believing husband. Otherwise your children would be unclean, but as it is, they are holy.

But if the unbeliever leaves, let him do so. A believing man or woman is not bound in such circumstances; God has called us to live in peace.

Ephesians 5:22–24

Wives, submit to your husbands as to the Lord. For the husband is the head of the wife as Christ is the head of the church, his body, of which he is the Savior. Now as the church submits to Christ, so also wives should submit to their husbands in everything.

Ephesians 5:25–33

Husbands, love your wives, just as Christ loved the church and gave himself up for her to make her holy, cleansing her by the washing with water through the word, and to present her to himself as a radiant church, without stain or wrinkle or any other blemish, but holy and blameless. In this same way, husbands ought to love their wives as their own bodies. He who loves his wife loves himself. After all, no one ever hated his own body, but he feeds and cares for it, just as Christ does the church—for we are members of his body. "For this reason a man will leave his father and mother and be united to his wife, and the two will become one flesh." This is a profound mystery—but I am talking about Christ and the church. However, each one of you also must love his wife as he loves himself, and the wife must respect her husband.

Ephesians 6:1–2

Children, obey your parents in the Lord, for this is right. "Honor your father and mother"—which is the first commandment with a promise—"that it may go well with you and that you may enjoy long life on the earth."

Ephesians 6:4

Fathers, do not exasperate your children; instead, bring them up in the training and instruction of the Lord.

Colossians 3:18

Wives, submit to your husbands, as is fitting in the Lord.

Colossians 3:19

Husbands, love your wives and do not be harsh with them.

Colossians 3:20

Children, obey your parents in everything, for this pleases the Lord.

Colossians 3:21

Fathers, do not embitter your children, or they will become discouraged.

1 Timothy 3:2

Now the overseer must be above reproach, the husband of but one wife. . . .

1 Timothy 3:12

A deacon must be the husband of but one wife and must manage his children and his household well.

Hebrews 13:4

Marriage should be honored by all, and the marriage bed kept pure, for God will judge the adulterer and all the sexually immoral.

1 Peter 3:1–6

Wives, in the same way be submissive to your husbands so that, if any of them do not believe the word, they may be won over without words by the behavior of their wives, when they see the purity and reverence of your lives. Your beauty should not come from outward adornment, such as braided hair and the wearing of gold jewelry and fine clothes. Instead, it should be that of your inner self, the unfading beauty of a gentle and quiet spirit, which is of great worth in God's sight. For this is the way the holy women of the past who put their hope in God used to make themselves beautiful. They were submissive to their own husbands, like Sarah, who obeyed Abraham and called him her master. You are her daughters if you do what is right and do not give away to fear.

1 Peter 3:7
Husbands, in the same way be considerate as you live with your wives, and treat them with respect as the weaker partner and as heirs with you of the gracious gift of life, so that nothing will hinder your prayers.

STUDY QUESTIONS AND EXERCISES

1. It is interesting that we see Jesus performing His first miracle at a wedding feast in Cana of Galilee (John 2:1–5). What miracle did He perform? What do Revelation 19:9 and 21:2 tell us about a future wedding feast? How is the marriage of a man and woman like that of Christ and His church?

2. Hosea is a book that speaks of God's covenant relationship with His people Israel. Read Hosea 2:19–3:3. Who is the unfaithful wife of chapter 3? Of whom does the Lord speak in 2:25?

3. What does Deuteronomy 11:19–20 teach us about instructing our children today? How are we to go about it?

4. What does Proverbs 27:15–16 have to say about a quarrelsome wife? In what respect is she disobeying the command of God?

5. According to 1 Peter 3:7, what might hinder the prayers of a husband? Why do you think this would hinder prayer?

More Verses to Ponder
Genesis 3:16; 18:19; Esther 1:20; Proverbs 19:13; 21:9, 19

A Verse to Memorize
"Marriage should be honored by all, and the marriage bed kept pure, for God will judge the adulterer and all the sexually immoral." (Heb. 13:4)

My Personal Action Plan to Honor Christ in My Family

1.

2.

3.

4.

Chapter 12

The Christian Church

Jesus said in John 15:12, "My command is this: Love each other as I have loved you." He repeated Himself in verse 17: "This is my command: Love each other."

I don't know about you and your local church, but I've found that some folks have a very strange way of displaying love. Love is the catalyst that brings peace and unity. Sin—the absence of godly love—brings division and conflict. Godly love—the love of Christ—is crucial if Christ's church is to live in peace and harmony. It should be the church's defining characteristic, flowing from our pure faith in the Savior. For Christ also said in John 13:35, "By this all men will know that you are my disciples, if you love one another."

$$\mathcal{A}$$

STRIVING FOR PEACE

Jesus said, "Blessed are the peacemakers, for they will be called sons of God" (Matt. 5:9). Ours is the God of peace. He is very concerned about peace, both spiritual and social.

Spiritual peace is that which Christ brings when He comes to dwell within us. It is "peace with God" (Rom. 5:1). Without this there is no lasting peace. Jesus said in John 14:27, "Peace I leave with you; my peace I give you. I do not give to you as the world gives. Do not let your hearts be troubled and do not be

afraid." God's peace is a peace that "transcends all understanding" (Phil. 4:7), guarding our hearts and minds in Christ
Jesus. For, "to be spiritually minded is life and peace" (Rom.
8:6 KJV).

Social peace—in our church, home, business, or community—is a peace that flows from a love for others that only God
can give. God's love is the glue that unites and bonds people
together. Pride, selfishness, envy, and other sins are the dynamite that explodes relationships.

Social peace is always subordinate to spiritual peace. We
must not get the cart before the horse. If there is no peace with
God, there can be no lasting peace in relationships.

Many Christians today believe that doctrine is the culprit
that brings disharmony in the church. That is simply not true.
It is not doctrine, but unbelief in proper doctrine that causes
the problem. Paul wrote, "The time will come when men will
not put up with sound doctrine. Instead, to suit their own desires, they will gather around them a great number of teachers
to say what their itching ears want to hear" (2 Tim. 4:3). That
time has come.

Doctrine, a true understanding of God and man, is essen-
tial to peace and harmony. Without it, the match is laid to the
dynamite's fuse. But proper doctrine should always foster humility. Otherwise good doctrine can be explosive too. As Paul
says in 1 Corinthians 8:1–2, "Knowledge puffs up, but love
builds up. The man who thinks he knows something does not
yet know as he ought to know." Those who embrace good
teaching should also embrace a compassionate, gentle, and
loving attitude toward others. If your attitude toward others is
rotted, your doctrine is too.

Mark 9:50
". . . be at peace with each other."

Romans 12:16a
Live in harmony with one another.

Romans 12:18

If it is possible, as far as it depends on you, live at peace with everyone.

Romans 14:19

Let us therefore make every effort to do what leads to peace and to mutual edification.

Romans 16:17

I urge you, brothers, to watch out for those who cause divisions and put obstacles in your way that are contrary to the teaching you have learned. Keep away from them.

1 Corinthians 1:10

I appeal to you, brothers, in the name of our Lord Jesus Christ, that all of you agree with one another so that there may be no divisions among you and that you may be perfectly united in mind and thought.

Ephesians 4:3

Make every effort to keep the unity of the Spirit through the bond of peace.

Philippians 2:14

Do everything without complaining or arguing. . . .

Colossians 3:12–14

Therefore as God's chosen people, holy and dearly loved, clothe yourselves with compassion, kindness, humility, gentleness and patience. Bear with each other and forgive whatever grievances you may have against one another. Forgive as the Lord forgave you. And over all these virtues put on love, which binds them all together in perfect unity.

Colossians 3:15

Let the peace of Christ rule in your hearts, since as members of one body you were called to peace. And be thankful.

1 Thessalonians 5:13b
Live in peace with each other.

2 Timothy 2:14
Keep reminding them of these things. Warn them before God against quarreling about words; it is of no value, and only ruins those who listen.

2 Timothy 2:22–26
Flee the evil desires of youth, and pursue righteousness, faith, love and peace, along with those who call on the Lord out of a pure heart. Don't have anything to do with foolish and stupid arguments, because you know they produce quarrels. And the Lord's servant must not quarrel; instead, he must be kind to everyone, able to teach, not resentful. Those who oppose him he must gently instruct, in the hope that God will grant them repentance leading them to a knowledge of the truth, and that they will come to their senses and escape from the trap of the devil, who has taken them captive to do his will.

Titus 3:9–11
But avoid foolish controversies and genealogies and arguments and quarrels about the law, because these are unprofitable and useless. Warn a divisive person once, and then warn him a second time. After that, have nothing to do with him. You may be sure that such a man is warped and sinful; he is self-condemned.

Hebrews 12:14
Make every effort to live at peace with all men and to be holy; without holiness no one will see the Lord.

1 Peter 3:8–9
Finally, all of you, live in harmony with one another; be sympathetic, love as brothers, be compassionate and humble. Do not repay evil with evil or insult with insult, but

with blessing, because to this you were called so that you may inherit a blessing.

STUDY QUESTIONS AND EXERCISES

1. Read Psalm 133. Find the references to both spiritual and social peace in this short psalm of ascents.

2. In Matthew 10:34–36, Jesus seems to refute what He has said about the blessedness of "peacemakers" earlier. In what ways does Jesus bring a sword, and not peace? Have you found Christianity to be a dividing issue in your home? In that circumstance, should your central desire be peace with God, or peace in your home?

3. Read Proverbs 16:7. In what way does this proverb show the priority of spiritual peace over social peace.

4. Read James 3:17–18. Where does James say that the wisdom that brings peace comes from? List the eight characteristics of this wisdom:

   (1)_____ (2)_____

   (3)_____ (4)_____

   (5)_____ (6)_____

   (7)_____ (8)_____

   What is the harvest for the peacemaker?

5. Consider your local church. Have there been problems with peace in the past? What was the central cause? What can be done in the future to avoid conflict?

6. Following up on question 2, above, what are some of the issues that may divide a church or a home? Is peace always preferable to division? Under what circumstances may it not be?

More Verses to Ponder
Psalm 34:14; 120:6–7; Proverbs 17:1; 20:3; Isaiah 2:4; 45:7

A Verse to Memorize
"I appeal to you, brothers, in the name of our Lord Jesus Christ, that all of you agree with one another so that there may be no divisions among you and that you may be perfectly united in mind and thought." (1 Cor. 1:10)

My Personal Action Plan to Be a Peacemaker

1.

2.

3.

4.

THE FAMILY OF GOD

God has provided believers with an extended family that transcends time and space. One day we will be reunited with loved ones we have never met, like great-great-grandfathers and -mothers, and yes, others we have known who have gone on to be with the Lord. What an indescribable joy to live eternally by their side!

But for the present we are in the flesh, and our church family is less than perfect. The Lord has given us guidelines to live together as His family, imperfect though we now are. Again, all of His commands direct us in this endeavor. These following specific commands are aimed at church members in relationship to others of the same precious faith.

My church home is wonderful. True, we have our share of sin and trials, but there is a deep sense of love and fellowship that visitors can spot immediately. My pastor and his wife set the tone. They are caring shepherds, who suffer when we suffer and rejoice when we rejoice. We truly care about one another and pray for one another, encouraging one another in the faith. Is your church home like that?

At the same time, I have never been in a church where the biblical teaching has been clearer, or the gospel given out more frequently. All of us in the family of God need the gospel preached to us regularly. We need to be reminded of what we were: dead in trespasses and sins, lost forever but for the grace of God. And, we need to be reminded of who God is: high and exalted, holy and just, but merciful and tender. He became a man, just like us, and paid the penalty so that we, by faith in His blood, might be justified in the Father's sight. By Christ's atoning work, we are born into an eternal family! Praise His wonderful name!

Romans 12:11–13

Never be lacking in zeal, but keep your spiritual fervor, serving the Lord. Be joyful in hope, patient in affliction, faithful in prayer. Share with God's people who are in need. Practice hospitality.

1 Corinthians 10:14

Therefore, my dear friends, flee from idolatry.

1 Corinthians 11:23–34a

For I received from the Lord what I also passed on to you: The Lord Jesus, on the night he was betrayed, took bread, and when he had given thanks, he broke it and said, "This is my body, which is for you; do this in remembrance of me." In the same way, after supper he took the cup, saying, "This cup is the new covenant in my blood; do this, whenever you drink it, in remembrance of me." For whenever you eat this bread and drink this cup, you proclaim the Lord's death until he comes."

Therefore, whoever eats the bread or drinks the cup of the Lord in an unworthy manner will be guilty of sinning against the body and blood of the Lord. A man ought to examine himself before he eats of the bread and drinks of the cup. For anyone who eats and drinks without recognizing the body of the Lord eats and drinks judgment on himself. That is why many among you are weak and sick, and a number of you have fallen asleep. But if we judged ourselves, we would not come under judgment. When we are judged by the Lord, we are being disciplined so that we will not be condemned with the world.

So then, my brothers, when you come together to eat, wait for each other. If anyone is hungry, he should eat at home, so that when you meet together it may not result in judgment.

2 Corinthians 6:14–18

Do not be yoked together with unbelievers. For what do righteousness and wickedness have in common? Or what fellowship can light have with darkness? What harmony is there between Christ and Belial? What does a believer have in common with an unbeliever? What agreement is there between the temple of God and idols? For we are the temple of the living God. As God has said: "I will live with them and walk among them, and I will be their God, and they will be my people."

"Therefore come out from them
    and be separate,
        says the Lord.

Touch no unclean thing,
and I will receive you."
"I will be a Father to you,
and you will be my sons and daughters,
says the Lord Almighty."

Galatians 6:1–2

Brothers, if someone is caught in a sin, you who are spiritual should restore him gently. But watch yourself, or you also may be tempted. Carry each others burdens, and in this way you will fulfill the law of Christ.

Galatians 6:9–10

Let us not become weary in doing good, for at the proper time we will reap a harvest if we do not give up. Therefore, as we have opportunity, let us do good to all people, especially to those who belong to the family of believers.

Ephesians 5:6–7

Let no one deceive you with empty words, for because of such things God's wrath comes on those who are disobedient. Therefore, do not be partners with them.

Ephesians 5:11–12

Have nothing to do with the fruitless deeds of darkness, but rather expose them. For it is shameful even to mention what the disobedient do in secret.

Colossians 3:16b

. . . teach and admonish one another with all wisdom. . . .

2 Thessalonians 3:6

In the name of the Lord Jesus Christ, we command you, brothers, to keep away from every brother who is idle and does not live according to the teaching you have received from us. [Cf. v. 14.]

1 Timothy 2:9–10
I also want women to dress modestly, with decency and propriety, not with braided hair or gold or pearls or expensive clothes, but with good deeds, appropriate for women who profess to worship God.

1 Timothy 2:11
A woman should learn in quietness and full submission.

1 Timothy 2:12
I do not permit a woman to teach or to have authority over a man; she must be silent.

1 Timothy 5:1–2
Do not rebuke an older man harshly, but exhort him as if he were your father. Treat younger men as brothers, older women as mothers, and younger women as sisters, with absolute purity.

1 Timothy 5:3–4
Give proper recognition to those widows who are really in need. But if a widow has children or grandchildren, these should learn first of all to put their religion into practice by caring for their own family and so repaying their parents and grandparents, for this is pleasing to God.

1 Timothy 5:22
Do not be hasty in the laying on of hands, and do not share in the sins of others. Keep yourself pure.

2 Timothy 3:5b
Have nothing to do with [those "having a form of godliness but denying its power."]

Titus 2:2
Teach the older men to be temperate, worthy of respect, self-controlled, and sound in faith, in love and in endurance.

Titus 2:3–5

Likewise, teach the older women to be reverent in the way they live, not to be slanderers or addicted to much wine, but to teach what is good. Then they can train the younger women to love their husbands and children, to be self-controlled and pure, to be busy at home, to be kind, and to be subject to their husbands, so that no one will malign the word of God.

Titus 2:6–8

Similarly, encourage the young men to be self-controlled. In everything set them an example by doing what is good. In your teaching show integrity, seriousness and soundness of speech that cannot be condemned, so that those who oppose you may be ashamed because they have nothing bad to say about us.

Hebrews 10:25a

Let us not give up meeting together, as some are in the habit of doing. . . .

Hebrews 12:28b–29

. . . and so worship God acceptably with reverence and awe, for our "God is a consuming fire."

Hebrews 13:16

And do not forget to do good and to share with others, for with such sacrifices God is pleased.

James 5:16a

Therefore confess your sins to each other. . . .

Study Questions and Exercises

1. In Revelation 1, John heard the voice of Christ speaking to him, and saw seven golden lampstands, representing the

seven churches. Read chapters 2 and 3, and write down what Christ says—good and bad—about each church. When finished, ask yourself what conclusions may be drawn. If you are in a study group, compare your findings with others'.

a. Ephesus:

Good

Bad

b. Smyrna:

Good

Bad

c. Pergamum:

Good

Bad

d. Thyratira:

Good

Bad

   e. Sardis:

      Good

      Bad

   f. Philadelphia:

      Good

      Bad

   g. Laodicea:

      Good

      Bad

2. In 2 Corinthians 6:14–18, Paul enjoins us against being un-
equally yoked with unbelievers. Usually we apply this in-
junction to the context of marriage or a business partner-

ship. What situation(s) in the local church might make the command about unequal yokes relevant there also?

3. One of the most precious parts of Christian worship is the Lord's Supper. In 1 Corinthians 11:22–34 Paul speaks of our participation in the sacrament and says some rather frightful words. For instance, in verse 27 he speaks of taking the Supper in an "unworthy manner." What does that mean? Does it have anything to do with "recognizing the body of the Lord" in verse 29?

More Verses to Ponder
Psalms 111:1; 125:1; 133:1; Isaiah 4:2–6; Ephesians 1:22–23

A Verse to Memorize
"Let us not give up meeting together, as some are in the habit of doing." (Heb. 10:25a)

My Personal Action Plan to Encourage the Saints and to Bring Peace in My Church

1.

2.

3.

4.

Chapter 13

The Christian and Holiness

Someone might ask of Christianity, "What's the big idea?" To my mind, the "big idea" of Christianity is that God—the Creator and Sustainer of the universe—is calling a people out of a sinful and godless world to be like Himself, to live with Him, and to glorify Him eternally. In other words, God is calling a holy people to Himself through the work of Jesus Christ. If we could only catch a glimpse of ourselves as sinners, we wouldn't be able to stand it. But we would never again cease to marvel at how a holy God could love such a filthy lot. God has called us to holiness and our response should be a willing submission to the Spirit's rule over our lives. That means glory to God who commands, and joy for the sinner who obeys.

SINS OF THE FLESH

Paul reminds us in Galatians 5:19–26 of the wide gap that exists between the sins of the flesh and the fruit of the Spirit. He says,

> The acts of the sinful nature are obvious: sexual immorality, impurity and debauchery; idolatry and witchcraft; hatred, discord, jealousy, fits of rage, selfish am-

bition, dissensions, factions and envy; drunkenness, orgies and the like. I warn you, as I did before, that those who live like this will not inherit the kingdom of God.

But the fruit of the Spirit is love, joy, peace, patience, kindness, goodness, faithfulness, gentleness and self-control. Against such things there is no law. Those who belong to Christ Jesus have crucified the sinful nature with its passions and desires. Since we live by the Spirit, let us keep in step with the Spirit. Let us not become conceited, provoking and envying each other.

Most of the following verses deal principally with sexual immorality and drunkenness. The other sins Paul mentions find expression in other verses listed in this volume. As you study these verses, concentrate on your action plan and the methods or mediums you will utilize to avoid the sins they describe.

Remember, "If you think you are standing firm, be careful that you don't fall! No temptation has seized you except what is common to man. And God is faithful; he will not let you be tempted beyond what you can bear. But when you are tempted, he will also provide a way out so that you can stand up under it" (1 Cor. 10:12–13).

Acts 15:19–20

It is my [Paul's] judgment, therefore, that we should not make it difficult for the Gentiles who are turning to God. Instead, we should write to them, telling them to abstain from food polluted by idols, from sexual immorality, from the meat of strangled animals and from blood.

Romans 13:13–14

Let us behave decently, as in the daytime, not in orgies and drunkenness, not in sexual immorality and debauchery, not in dissension and jealousy. Rather, clothe yourselves with the Lord Jesus Christ, and do not think about how to gratify the desires of the sinful nature.

1 Corinthians 6:18–20
Flee from sexual immorality. All other sins a man commits are outside his body, but he who sins sexually sins against his own body. Do you not know that your body is a temple of the Holy Spirit, who is in you, whom you have received from God? You are not your own; you were bought at a price. Therefore honor God with your body.

1 Corinthians 10:7
Do not be idolaters, as some of [the desert wanderers] were; as it is written: "The people sat down to eat and drink and got up to engage in pagan revelry."

1 Corinthians 10:8–9
We should not commit sexual immorality, as some of [the desert wanderers] did—and . . . were killed by snakes.

Ephesians 5:3
But among you there must not be even a hint of sexual immorality, or of any kind of impurity, or of greed, because these are improper for God's holy people.

Colossians 3:5
Put to death, therefore, whatever belongs to your earthly nature: sexual immorality, impurity, lust, evil desires and greed, which is idolatry.

1 Thessalonians 4:3–7
It is God's will that you should be sanctified; that you should avoid sexual immorality; that each of you should learn to control his own body in a way that is holy and honorable, not in passionate lust like the heathen, who do not know

God; and that in this matter no one should wrong his brother or take advantage of him. The Lord will punish men for all such sins, as we have already told you and warned you. For God did not call us to be impure, but to live a holy life.

1 Thessalonians 5:6–8

So then, let us not be like others, who are asleep, but let us be alert and self-controlled. For those who sleep, sleep at night, and those who get drunk, get drunk at night. But since we belong to the day, let us be self-controlled, putting on love and faith as a breastplate, and the hope of salvation as a helmet.

Hebrews 12:16

See that no one is sexually immoral, or is godless like Esau, who for a single meal sold his inheritance rights as the oldest son.

STUDY QUESTIONS AND EXERCISES

1. In 1 Corinthians 5:1–13, Paul notes a serious problem in the Corinthian church. What is it? Why is Paul so concerned about it, beyond the sinner's own soul? What does he tell them to do?

2. Read Proverbs 5, 6, and 7. Of what sins are we warned in these chapters? What ways are we given to escape them? Where does the path lead for the victim of the adulteress?

3. Ephesians 5:3 speaks of a "hint" of immorality. What is Paul talking about? How do we "hint" of immorality? How can we avoid it? Might our attempt to obey this command cause us to add to the law of God by imposing stricter standards on others than we should?

4. Colossians 3:5 speaks of greed being idolatry. How is that so? Could any other sins be considered to be tantamount to idolatry? Which ones and why?

More Verses to Ponder
Proverbs 22:14; Matthew 5:28; 15:19; James 2:11; Romans 1:28–32

A Verse to Memorize
"Put to death, therefore, whatever belongs to your earthly nature: sexual immorality, impurity, lust, evil desires and greed, which is idolatry." (Col. 3:5)

My Personal Action Plan to Flee from Sins of the Flesh

1.

2.

3.

4.

B

GENERAL PRECEPTS FOR HOLY LIVING

The Lord our God is a holy God. He demands His people to be the same. He says, "Be holy, because I am holy" (Lev. 11:44–45; 1 Peter 1:16). What does it mean to be holy?

First, holiness for God means to be set apart, to be distinct from and transcendent above His creation. But God is also morally holy, and it is to this holiness that God calls you and me. Here's what *The Evangelical Dictionary of Theology* (ed. Walter A. Elwell [Grand Rapids: Baker, 1984], 455) says about God's moral holiness:

> God is morally spotless in character and action, upright, pure, and untainted with evil desires, motives, thought, words, or acts. God is holy, and as such is the source and standard of what is right. God is free from all evil, loves all truth and goodness. He values purity and detests impurity and inauthenticity. . . . Holiness is not solely the product of God's will, but a changeless characteristic of his eternal nature.

Holiness is what this whole book has been about. These last few verses are general calls to holiness and obedience that were not easily classified elsewhere. I hope you will dwell on them, soaking up their truths, all the while reveling in the God who gave them to us.

Matthew 5:33–37

"Again, you have heard that it was said to the people long ago, 'Do not break your oath, but keep the oaths you have made to the Lord.' But I tell you, Do not swear at all: either by heaven, for it is God's throne; or by the earth, for it is his footstool; or by Jerusalem, for it is the city of the Great King. And do not swear by your head, for you cannot make even one hair white or black. Simply let your 'Yes' be 'Yes,' and your 'No,' 'No'; anything beyond this comes from the evil one."

Romans 12:9b

Hate what is evil; cling to what is good.

2 Corinthians 7:1

Since we have these promises, dear friends, let us purify ourselves from everything that contaminates body and spirit, perfecting holiness out of reverence for God.

2 Corinthians 13:5

Examine yourselves to see whether you are in the faith; test yourselves.

2 Corinthians 13:11a

Finally, brothers, good-by. Aim for perfection. . . .

Galatians 5:16

So, I say, live by the Spirit, and you will not gratify the desires of the sinful nature.

Galatians 5:19–21

The acts of the sinful nature are obvious: sexual immorality, impurity and debauchery; idolatry and witchcraft; hatred, discord, jealousy, fits of rage, selfish ambition, dissensions, factions and envy; drunkenness, orgies, and the like. I warn you, as I did before, that those who live like this will not inherit the kingdom of God.

Ephesians 4:22–23

You were taught, with regard to your former way of life, to put off your old self, which is being corrupted by its deceitful desires; to be made new in the attitude of your minds; and to put on the new self, created to be like God in true righteousness and holiness.

Ephesians 5:1

Be imitators of God, therefore, as dearly loved children. . . .

Ephesians 5:15–17

Be very careful then, how you live—not as unwise but wise, making the most of every opportunity, because the days are evil. Therefore do not be foolish, but understand what the Lord's will is.

Ephesians 5:18

Do not get drunk on wine, which leads to debauchery. Instead, be filled with the Spirit.

Philippians 1:27

Whatever happens, conduct yourselves in a manner worthy of the gospel of Christ.

Philippians 4:9

Whatever you have learned or received or heard from me, or seen in me—put it into practice. And the God of peace will be with you.

1 Thessalonians 4:11a

Make it your ambition to lead a quiet life, to mind your own business. . . .

1 Thessalonians 5:14–15

And we urge you, brothers, warn those who are idle, encourage the timid, help the weak, be patient with everyone. Make sure that nobody pays back wrong for wrong, but always try to be kind to each other and to everyone else.

1 Thessalonians 5:22

Avoid every kind of evil.

1 Timothy 4:12b

Set an example for the believers in speech, in life, in love, in faith and in purity.

1 Timothy 5:21

. . . keep these instructions without partiality, and . . . do nothing out of favoritism.

1 Timothy 6:11

But you, man of God, flee from all this [sin], and pursue righteousness, godliness, faith, love, endurance and gentleness.

2 Timothy 2:22
Flee the evil desires of youth, and pursue righteousness, faith, love and peace, along with those who call on the Lord out of a pure heart.

Titus 3:8
This is a trustworthy saying. And I want you to stress these things, so that those who have trusted in God may be careful to devote themselves to doing what is good. These things are excellent and profitable for everyone.

Hebrews 12:1
Therefore, since we are surrounded by such a great cloud of witnesses, let us throw off everything that hinders and the sin that so easily entangles, and let us run with perseverance the race marked out for us.

Hebrews 12:7a
Endure hardship as discipline; God is treating you as sons.

Hebrews 12:14
Make every effort to live at peace with all men and to be holy; without holiness no one will see the Lord.

James 1:21
Therefore, get rid of all moral filth and the evil that is so prevalent and humbly accept the word planted in you, which can save you.

James 1:27b
Keep [your]self from being polluted by the world.

James 2:1
My brothers, as believers in our glorious Lord Jesus Christ, don't show favoritism.

James 3:13

Who is wise and understanding among you? Let him show it by his good life, by deeds done in the humility that comes from wisdom.

James 4:7–10

Submit yourselves, then, to God. Resist the devil, and he will flee from you. Come near to God and he will come near to you. Wash your hands, you sinners, and purify your hearts, you double-minded. Grieve, mourn and wail. Change your laughter to mourning and your joy to gloom. Humble yourselves before the Lord, and he will lift you up.

1 Peter 1:13

Therefore, prepare your minds for action; be self-controlled; set your hope fully on the grace to be given you when Jesus Christ is revealed.

1 Peter 1:16

For it is written: "Be holy, because I am holy."

1 Peter 2:1

Therefore, rid yourselves of all malice and all deceit, hypocrisy, envy, and slander of every kind.

1 Peter 2:11–12

Dear friends, I urge you, as aliens and strangers in the world, to abstain from sinful desires, which war against your soul. Live such good lives among the pagans that, although they accuse you of doing wrong, they may see your good deeds and glorify God on the day he visits us.

1 Peter 4:7

The end of all things is near. Therefore be clear minded and self-controlled so that you can pray.

2 Peter 3:11–12a

Since everything will be destroyed in this way, what kind of people ought you to be? You ought to live holy and godly lives as you look forward to the day of God and speed its coming.

1 John 2:15–17

Do not love the world or anything in the world. If anyone loves the world, the love of the Father is not in him. For everything in the world—the cravings of sinful man, the lust of his eyes and the boasting of what he has and does—comes not from the Father but from the world. The world and its desires pass away, but the man who does the will of God lives forever.

3 John 11

Dear friend, do not imitate what is evil but what is good. Anyone who does what is good is from God. Anyone who does what is evil has not seen God.

STUDY QUESTIONS AND EXERCISES

1. In Matthew 5:33–37, Jesus warns us about oath-taking. Is He saying that we shouldn't swear an oath in court that we will "tell the truth, the whole truth, and nothing but the truth"? Why is He concerned with the swearing of oaths? If you are in a study group, discuss this with others (along with the rest of the questions in this section).

2. Paul says in 1 Corinthians 13:5, "Examine yourselves to see whether you are in the faith." How do we do this? What things should we be looking for? What relationship does this verse have to his statement in Philippians 2:12?

3. Read Galatians 5:16. How do we "live by the Spirit"? What can we do to ensure that we will be constantly living by Him? How do we recognize when we're not?

4. 2 Timothy 2:22 instructs us to "flee the evil desires of youth." What is it about youth that leads many to act foolishly, even though they may know the Lord? What does wisdom have to do with an understanding of the consequences of some course of action? How can we effectively instruct young people to "pursue righteousness"?

5. James instructs us to "keep [ourselves] from being polluted by the world" (James 1:27). What are some practical ways of doing that, short of withdrawing from the world altogether?

A Verse to Memorize

"Since we have these promises, dear friends, let us purify ourselves from everything that contaminates body and spirit, perfecting holiness out of reverence for God." (2 Cor. 7:1)

My Personal Action Plan to Live a Holy Life Before God

1.

2.

3.

4.

For Further Study of the Ten Commandments

Coffman, James B. *The Ten Commandments, Yesterday and Today.* Westwood, N.J.: Revell, 1996.

Douma, J. *The Ten Commandments: Manual for the Christian Life.* Translated by Nelson D. Kloosterman. Phillipsburg, N.J.: P&R Publishing, 1996.

Rushdoony, Rousas John. *The Institutes of Biblical Law.* Phillipsburg, N.J.: Presbyterian and Reformed, 1978.

Simcox, Carroll E. *Living the Ten Commandments.* New York: Morehouse-Goreham, 1953.

Weatherly, Owen M. *The Ten Commandments in Modern Perspective.* Richmond, Va.: John Knox Press, 1961.